Talking Texts

Talking Texts

A Teachers' Guide to
Book Clubs across the Curriculum

Lesley Roessing

Foreword by
Lester Laminack

ROWMAN & LITTLEFIELD
Lanham • Boulder • New York • London

Published by Rowman & Littlefield
A wholly owned subsidiary of The Rowman & Littlefield Publishing Group, Inc.
4501 Forbes Boulevard, Suite 200, Lanham, Maryland 20706
www.rowman.com

Unit A, Whitacre Mews, 26-34 Stannary Street, London SE11 4AB

British Library Cataloguing in Publication Information Available

Library of Congress Cataloging-in-Publication Data

ISBN 978-1-4758-3457-4 (cloth : alk. paper)
ISBN 978-1-4758-3458-1 (paper : alk. paper)
ISBN 978-1-4758-3459-8 (electronic)

To all the educators willing to attempt new strategies and practices to help their readers and writers grow and to the students they serve. To my grandsons, Dean and Max, who, I hope, will be inspired and encouraged by such teachers.

Contents

~

Foreword

Lester Laminack

"No man can reveal to you aught but that which already lies half asleep in the dawning of your knowledge. The teacher who walks in the shadow of the temple, among his followers, gives not of his wisdom but rather of his faith and his lovingness. If he is indeed wise he does not bid you enter the house of his wisdom, but rather leads you to the threshold of your own mind."

—Kahlil Gibran (*The Prophet*)

I believe it is a safe bet to assume you have seen a movie that moved you in some way. It may have left you stunned and utterly speechless. Perhaps you were brought to tears. Or maybe, you were seething with anger. That movie may have taken you back to an event in your life that left you terrified, or overjoyed, or tingling with overwhelming new feelings. Whether you attended that movie alone or went to the theater with friends, you most likely left the theater feeling the need to talk about it. If you were alone, you may have called or texted a family member or friend. You may have turned to social media. If you were with friends, you may have gone to dinner, or out for drinks, just to talk about it. There is a strong need to reach out, to connect with others when moved by an experience with story, information, language . . . text of any kind.

Through social interaction we are able to float our thoughts and perceptions, to test our theories, to share our take on the characters—their motives, actions, reactions, and outcomes. We need a place to test our thinking, to offer our initial reactions to the events, to challenge the setting, or praise the development of tension. Likewise, we seek those outlets to express our sense of right and wrong, to share our sense of moral outrage, to gauge reactions to notions we wish to challenge when the movie is a nonfiction presentation (e.g., a documentary or biography). Often we leave these heady, and sometimes heated, conversations with an altered perspective. We may step into the conversation with one attitude and leave with another. We may enter the conversation staunchly defending one character and find that our notions of that character shift quite a bit as we hear what others have to say. We may lead the conversation arguing the facts were inaccurate only to discover that we have lived with inaccuracies as "our truth" for years.

The power of talk bubbling up naturally among adults who have seen the same movie is something that most of us have experienced for ourselves. The talk nudges us to consider other perspectives, to place our tentative theories and attitudes on hold long enough to listen to the thoughts of another. The more respect we have for the others in these conversations, the more likely we are to pause, reflect, and reconsider our own initial thinking. As adults we recognize that these conversations generally lead us to a more robust understanding of the topic, deeper insights, and more diverse perspectives. It is through those conversations that we have the opportunity to test, refine, and outgrow our own provincialism. It is because of these conversations that we bring more to our next experience with a movie. And, as a result of these experiences, our conversations about the next movie are deeper, more insightful, and more robust.

Now, if you are a reader, chances are that you have had similar urges and experiences with books, articles, essays, poetry, blog posts, and almost every form of print you have engaged in. You know that you will grow your insights and understandings by talking with others who have read the same texts.

We know the power of these conversations. We are the beneficiaries of that power, yet too few of our classrooms tap into it for our students. Imagine the impact of having small groups of students engaging in the same text, having time to sit with it and reflect, think, and write, and then come together to talk. Imagine they come together to talk about text in the same way you have talked with others about a movie. There is no set of questions to log on and answer. There are no vocabulary words to look up and use in a sentence. Instead, there is chomping at the bits, unbridled and powerful talk guided only by what this small band of readers finds compelling.

Lesley Roessing understands the power of that kind of engagement with texts of all types. She has firsthand knowledge of what happens when young readers and writers are given permission to delve in and pursue their insights and confusions in a text they are reading as a group. Lesley has helped students across grade levels develop the skills and strategies needed to take charge of these conversations with grace and independence. The results are richly rewarding.

Lesley does not prescribe "the" way to develop and run book clubs in the classroom. She does not lay out a rigid set of guidelines for the correct way to include book clubs in your curriculum. Instead, she acknowledges that this is not a new idea and builds off the work that has come before her. In her own classrooms, she has fine-tuned her thinking and honed her practices. Now, in this very accessible volume, she offers her finest thinking. She provides specific suggestions, guidelines, and rubrics within classroom examples. In short, she brings you into the conversation and invites you to take what works with your students within the parameters of your classroom. If the idea of book or text clubs is new to you, then you'll find comfort in the level of specificity. You'll relish the charts and rubrics offered as guidance. If your classroom has established book clubs up and running, then you'll find points of validation and will likely find several new twists to fine-tune your work. In this well-organized and accessible book, Lesley offers a powerful resource that can transform how your students think about reading.

~

Acknowledgments

I am grateful for my British literature seniors at Interboro High School about whom I write in the introduction. That first-ever class challenged me to analyze and apply the pedagogy and develop the methods I had just learned in my M.Ed. program to push myself to become the teacher they deserved, a process that I have continued for thirty years.

I am so very appreciative of the eighteen years with my former students at Ridley Middle School who inspired me to discover, create, and attempt new strategies to become a stronger teacher for them. They were continually willing to go along with my "newfangled" ideas, and they supported me in writing my first journal articles and professional books featuring their work to demonstrate what motivated, engaged students can achieve.

I thank the many K–12 teachers who have invited me into their classrooms to work with their students, especially those who have allowed me to facilitate book clubs. Joy Worrell, Brittany Zimniewicz, Holly Mills, and Elise Segally trusted me with their reading and social studies students. Those teachers allowed me to introduce book clubs, choose and book-talk novels, and teach social skills, discussion techniques, and daily focus lessons through the 9/11 Novel Study unit described in chapter 10. My colleagues and good friends Donna Martin and Heather Brougham-Cook have shared many, many classes with me over the years, inviting me to facilitate 9/11 book clubs, memoir book clubs, and verse-novel book clubs, as well as other literacy units of study.

I learned from the many teachers who passed through the Coastal Savannah Writing Project workshops and institutes in the ten years I directed—especially those who laughed and learned with me through the Summer Reading Institutes—and I hope I enthused many of them to not only undertake book or text clubs in their schools or classrooms but also to expand on the ideas I demonstrated and shared.

And I am now learning from the dedicated, hardworking faculty of Riverview Charter School—teachers who encourage me to join their classrooms and introduce book clubs and many other reading-writing-speaking lessons, and teachers who are open to new ideas and willing to share not only their strategies but also their students.

In addition, I am grateful for Rowman & Littlefield's Tom Koerner and Carlie Wall who graciously accepted my entreaties of "not ready yet" so I could get this handbook right, visiting more classrooms to create new response forms (see the appendix) to help readers reflect on their reading and prepare their thoughts for discussion as I practiced "just one more" strategy with students.

Last, I thank my family members who have supported my thirty-year passion for helping young readers become better, lifelong readers and, most important, for helping those students find the joy in reading.

Introduction

Thirty years ago I began my first teaching position. I taught five different high school classes, one being a British literature course. As a new teacher, I tried to faithfully follow the district's curriculum, not asking any questions. The course curriculum guide stated that I was to teach a Charles Dickens novel. I looked around the classroom; there were no class sets of any Dickens novel anywhere. *What to do?* I found four copies of *Oliver Twist*, a few copies of *Great Expectations*, and one old *David Copperfield*, and an idea was born. It was not important to teach a particular Dickens novel—or to *teach* a novel—but to expose the students to Dickens, his writings, the historical-social-economic time period in which the novels take place, and the issues presented in his writings.

We would all read Dickens, but we didn't have to read the same novel. So, I located, borrowed, and bought five copies of five different Dickens novels. Then I asked the students to look through the novels and rate their preferences. Based on their choices, I divided the class into five collaborative reading groups, or book clubs, giving each group copies of one novel.

After activating any prior knowledge the students had about Dickens or his time period, I provided necessary background information on Dickens, the history and economics of his time period, and his writing through lectures—it was the 1980s; today background information would be obtained by the students themselves through inquiry, research, and short presentations or publications that benefit the entire class, such as a "Dickens for Dummies" guide (Roessing, 2007). Then students were ready to form their book clubs and plan their reading.

Since students read at different rates and the novels are of differing lengths and posed diverse reading and discussion challenges, each group planned its own reading schedule; I merely provided a target completion date. Every other day the book clubs met for critical discussions and reflections on the chapters read—characters, setting, plot elements and twists, themes, and a few general questions I would throw out as I wandered from group to group. Students submitted their reading notes and their discussions notes so that I could keep track of their reading and meetings.

When all groups had finished their novels, each group collaboratively prepared a creative presentation to the class. In this way, all students could benefit from the five novels. I still remember the telethon for abandoned and orphaned children that tracked the exploits of little Oliver through phone calls made to the telethon by people who had spotted or interacted with the young man in his adventures, chronologically throughout the novel. In between phone calls, the book club members supplied us with researched information and statistics on homelessness, abandoned children, and runaways of both the Victorian era and contemporary times.

This was long before I read about book clubs or took part in my own adult book clubs. However, I noted not only the degree of engagement but also the collaboration of the readers in interpreting passages and meaning, as they, in parts, struggled with the text.

That first book club functioned smoothly and successfully, but it was 1989, and my class was composed of seventeen- and eighteen-year-old honors students; neither motivation nor behavior was an issue because they realized the reading and discussions were preparing them for college.

Years later in my own middle-grade heterogeneous classrooms, I again included small-group collaborative reading—literature circles and book clubs—in my curriculum as a bridge between reading whole-class common texts and individual self-selected reading.

However, I found I could not merely divide classes into groups and expect collaborative small-group reading to work as seamlessly as in that class of 1989 or at all. I learned that I needed to structure carefully, guiding my students through the transition to relative independence and the collaboration of small-group reading. I needed to teach multiple social skills and cooperation lessons and then coach students to prepare for and implement collaborative discussions.

Also, while I retained the Reading Workshop format with daily focus lessons that I had been employing for whole-class shared reading, I needed to adjust the format and lessons to accommodate book club reading. I scaffolded students gently though the transition, creating and teaching reader response lessons now tailored to encourage rich, thought-provoking conversations.

There is a dual purpose of book clubs. The first is to educate students to work collaboratively within a small group to accomplish specified goals. And the second objective—reading, comprehending, and synthesizing a text—I find is reached more effectively through successful collaboration.

Small-group collaborative reading, when executed effectively, engages all readers not only in the text but also in the ensuing student-centered discussions, increasing comprehension and adding to their reading, speaking, writing, and listening vocabularies. All readers, from "basic" to "proficient" readers, can then read books that are more challenging. Book clubs engage even reluctant readers, at all ages, because this way of reading is collaborative, social, and supportive.

Over the years, I have incorporated book clubs in a variety of academic settings and in multiple disciplines from elementary grades through university graduate classes. I have also widened the scope of the traditional book club by inaugurating book clubs in diverse formats—not only book clubs reading novels and memoirs but also article and poetry clubs, textbook clubs, and informational-text clubs.

The power of book clubs is undeniable. In one of my last years teaching eighth grade, some students came to me the last day of school. They were going into Level One History the next year and were assigned summer reading. The text was a nonfiction book that past students had told them was rather boring and difficult to comprehend. They were dreading reading it, and they asked me what they could do.

I thought for a moment and suggested, "You could form a summer book club to discuss the book *as* you all read it. You could meet once or twice a week and plan your reading and discussions. Also, remember that you reflected that your reader response journal helped you read better and deeper, so continue with writing response." They said goodbye and skipped off, pleased with that solution.

I wrote this book to serve as a handbook for teachers who want to employ small-group collaborative reading (book clubs) in their classrooms, augment their current teaching strategies to make small-group reading more effective, or extend the use of the book club format in other content areas or with other types of text (text clubs). My hope is that educators are inspired to include book clubs in their classes and that their students respond as enthusiastically as mine.

~

CHAPTER ONE

Defining School Book Clubs

They sit in circles, at tables, or on floor pillows. Each group of five students has the same novel in front of them. Group members are talking excitedly about characters, issues, conflicts, and decisions. As they chat, they look at notes in their reading journals and page through their novels. In one group, a student walks over to the world map on the classroom wall and points out a city in a far-away country. "That's where he came from; that's the setting in the last chapter," he exclaims. The others nod, taking in how far their protagonist had to travel to come to the United States. This is a book club in action.

A book club is composed of a small collaborative group of readers. Within their book club, readers read the same book and discuss that book. Many are familiar with the typical adult book clubs where members choose a book or one of the members chooses a book that all members will read for the next meeting. Each member reads the book individually, and all readers then meet once, after reading, to discuss the book. In some book clubs, a member serves as a facilitator to introduce the author and the book, perhaps conducting and presenting some background research on the author, book, and topic. This format has been adapted for schools and can be implemented in any grade level and discipline.

What Is a Book Club?

There are many types of book clubs, but the main components remain the same no matter what type of text, genre, or format is read—fiction texts, narrative-nonfiction texts, informative texts in the form of novels, informational books, articles, short stories, plays, or poetry. Chapters 2 though 8 will focus primarily on fiction book clubs held in English/language arts classes; however, novels can also be employed in other content areas, and the same strategies and lessons can be taught with any text in any discipline and grade level. When referring to the collaborative, small-group reading of books, generally the term "book clubs" will be used; when discussing the collaborative reading of a variety of text types, the term "text clubs" will be used. Adaptations for text club reading of diverse types of texts in all disciplines will be discussed in detail in chapter 9.

In each book club, small groups of students read a book—or a collection of texts on one topic—and meet regularly for discussion throughout the time the text is being read. After the texts and discussions are concluded, the members of each book club share texts read with the entire class through a collaborative prepared presentation.

Book Clubs vs. Literature Circles

Although the terms can be used interchangeably, some teachers differentiate between literature circle and book club experiences. The term "literature circles"—or "text circles," or even "reading circles"—is fitting when the whole class is reading a common text but students meet in small, ongoing collaborative discussion groups. The term "book clubs" refers to groups that are each reading and discussing a different text.

In this way, literature circles can be employed as training, or rehearsal, for book clubs. Because students are all reading the same text, the teacher can control the reading schedule and can move students from group to group, if necessary or desired, for divergent discussion experiences.

Literature, or text, circles can be introduced three-fourths of the way through a shared novel or other chaptered text, after students have learned, reviewed, and applied multiple reading strategies and learned and practiced reader response strategies. Students are assigned to small groups, either randomly or by design, to discuss the current chapters of their shared text. In these literature circles, readers can be introduced to a variety of techniques that they will employ in their book club meetings. They remain in these circles for the remainder of the text, for one to two meetings, rehearsing for book club reading and collaboration.

Features of a Text Club

1. Students choose their own reading materials from appropriate choices provided or suggested by the teacher.
2. Small temporary groups are formed, based upon text choice. Students remain in a text club until the texts or collection of texts have been read, discussed, and shared.
3. Different text clubs read different texts. The texts for all the class text clubs may be the same type (e.g., fiction, memoir, or informative), the same format (e.g., books, articles, poetry, short stories, memoirs, or narratives), the same genre (e.g., prose, verse, or graphic), or centered on the same general topic or theme.
4. Text clubs meet on a regular predictable schedule to discuss their reading. Text clubs can meet every other day, allowing for reading days in between; two or three times a week; or once a week.
5. Each text club plans its own reading schedule, mindful of meeting dates and the projected end date. Some readers prefer reading less at the beginning of a text and then read faster as they become familiar with the text; some text clubs prefer reading more over weekends, and others prefer reading less over weekends. Reading schedules can be adjusted as the members read and meet. Many times readers find they are reading faster than expected, or, at other times, they may need to slow down their reading.
6. Discussions are student led, and topics come from group members. Discussions are guided by reader response notes, written individually during reading (see chapter 5). The goal is for meetings to be open, natural conversations about texts; therefore, personal connections, digressions, and open-ended questions are encouraged.
7. The teacher serves as text club facilitator, not as instructor or a text club member, during meetings. Teachers present whole-class focus lessons to facilitate reading comprehension and content knowledge and then listen in on club meetings to note participation, discussion skills and topics, and text references.
8. Evaluation and assessment is based on reader response journals and by teacher observation of discussions and by student self-evaluation. Grading can be based on individual journals and group after-reading presentations or publications (see chapter 7 on assessment).

Advantages of Text Club Reading

When readers read in text clubs, reading comprehension is increased. There are a variety of reasons for this increase in comprehension.

Research confirms that student motivation is a key factor in successful reading. The most fundamental advantage to text club reading is engagement because readers have a choice in their reading. When students are given choice of any kind, interest is enhanced, motivation and engagement are increased, and a positive attitude toward the assignment or activity results. In text club reading, students have some degree of choice in what they read; they can choose texts that interest them and with which they feel comfortable.

Book club reading is differentiation at work. When students choose books with which they feel comfortable and in which they are interested, the reading is differentiated for them. And they are members of groups who are comfortable with that same text reading level and hold the same interests as they have.

There is more motivation to read and more enjoyment of, or satisfaction with, reading in small-group collaborative situations. Readers can choose the focus of their conversations about the book, rather than merely answering questions the teacher has prepared. When members choose the points of discussion, conversation is more natural and engaging. Readers reveal what they find important to *them* in a text, leading to a more comprehensive exchange of ideas and deeper discourse.

Text clubs are social. Humans, especially children and adolescents, are, by their very nature, social beings. There has been much research that recognizes student social relationships as a potential agent for the improvement of student achievement.

Text club work is collaborative. Research has shown that people working together persisted longer on a challenging task, expressed greater interest in and enjoyment of the task, required less self-regulatory effort to persist on the task, and became more engrossed in and performed better on the task (Carr and Walton, 2014). The key to productive collaboration is purpose. In text clubs, students are collaborating and cooperating on shared goals—reading, understanding, and sharing a text—giving members a sense of purpose.

Since students are involved in a group project (reading) and have chosen that group because of a common interest in the text, they are participating in an environment where they feel welcome and accepted. In a text club, students are working toward a common goal, and, by planning the reading schedule and facilitating their own discussions, they have control over their learning, which research shows increases motivation and, therefore, engagement. With the smaller numbers, all members have not only a chance but also an obligation to actively contribute and move the conversation along.

Students are also motivated to actually read so that they can take an active part in text club meetings. There is a degree of peer pressure in being prepared for each meeting. Students will not tolerate members who are not prepared to contribute to meetings and presentations and expect others to do the work. Some text clubs refuse to allow members to participate in meetings if they do not bring their response journals, demonstrating that they have read and are ready to take part and contribute. In one classroom, the teacher noticed that a student was sitting in a corner of the room, away from her club, reading her book. When she was asked why she was not with her group, Lisa said, "This is the second time I have come to club unprepared. My group told me that I can't come back until I catch up with my reading." She read for the rest of the period. The act of reading increases reading comprehension.

Text clubs are inclusive. In text club discussions, multiple, diverse perspectives are encouraged and appreciated, which is another advantage. Unless based on a miscue, there are no "wrong" answers or insignificant points. Everyone is equal, and the small-group environment encourages everyone to speak. When asked, students have asserted that hearing multiple viewpoints from their peers is the most interesting part of text clubs and being able to share their personal perspectives is the most fun.

Since text club members are required to bring written notes to the meetings, readers are writing in response to text read, and in so doing, reflecting more on what they read. A 2010 report commissioned by the Carnegie Corporation, *Writing to Read: Evidence for How Writing Can Improve Reading* (Graham and Hebert, 2010), listed three core instructional practices effective in improving student reading. The first instructional practice listed is to "have students write about the texts they read." Depending on the types of response taught and assigned by the teacher or chosen by the reader, diverse reading and comprehension strategies are employed by readers. A variety of text club reader response strategies and journals will be introduced in chapter 5, and adaptations will be incorporated throughout this book.

Text club reading is more interactive. Comprehension is also increased simply because readers have the opportunities to discuss the reading with their peers. Many students have acknowledged that text clubs are advantageous because when readers do not understand something that they are reading, other members of their text club can explain when they meet. Students are more willing to share what they didn't understand with a small group than with an entire class.

This is even true when comprehension is compromised because a word or concept was missed when reading or a miscue caused comprehension to decrease. A text club was discussing a character in a novel, and one reader frowned and said, "I thought he died in the last chapter." All the students immediately opened their novels to check whether they had misread or what could have led Jake to that conclusion. Jake was the first to notice. "Oh, it says, 'I was so embarrassed; I wished I was dead.' How could I have read it wrong? I am glad he's not dead!" Jake said that the fact that all text club members went immediately to their books to check, instead of ridiculing him, made him feel that his comment was taken seriously and that he was a valued member of the group.

Also, when all members do not comprehend a part of the text, they have time to work out meaning and develop ideas together. Teachers have found that, because of the discussions and the collaborative nature of text clubs, students in text clubs can read more complex texts than they could individually.

Another benefit is that readers learn from, and about, the texts they are reading in clubs. Because meetings center on talk about text, readers cooperate in making meaning, clarifying confusions, and constructing ideas together. Readers not only remember and retain more about texts they take the time to analyze through member-led discussion, but more important, they also learn more from those texts.

Last, text clubs promote peer relationships and teach collaboration, teaching not only academic, but affective, learning skills. In text club meetings, students are working together to read, comprehend, gain meaning from a text, and share the text with others through after-reading synthesis. When students create understandings and build knowledge together, a sense of belonging and classroom community is created. Effective collaboration is one of the most important skills teachers can teach students for future participation as citizens.

CHAPTER TWO

~

Setting Up Book Clubs

Students sit in short rows or at tables of five or six. A bookshelf of the just-finished class novel, The Giver, *is in the back of the room. Students each have a different book in their hands and are scanning the covers or opening the books and reading a page. The books are all novels; some are written in prose, some are graphic novels, and one choice is a verse novel. They all have cover art or titles that somehow relate to dystopian societies. Some students smile and write down the titles of the books they are holding; others shake their heads and get ready to pass the book. One student holds up her book and points to a friend across the room. They pass their books to the next student. Students are getting ready to form book clubs.*

When setting up class book clubs, there are three main considerations: choosing the books, creating the reading groups, and planning when to include a book club in the curriculum.

Factors in Choosing Books for Book Clubs

The first consideration should be including a variety of diverse books. Variety can be based on reading levels, length, writing styles, genres, formats, topics or subtopics, and perspectives on the topics. Diversity can be based on the authors, the characters in a fictional text or the real individuals involved in a nonfiction text, or the settings or locales encompassed.

One primary reason for reading in book clubs is that students read at different reading levels, although reading level can very likely be dependent on background knowledge rather than a static proficiency level. Students will read at different levels contingent on their prior knowledge of, and interest in, the topic of the text. For example, a student who knows a lot about, or has experience playing or observing a sport, may have deeper understanding of sports fiction and nonfiction texts about sports than one who has no interest or background in the topic. No matter what type of text is chosen or what other considerations in selection are made, texts for book club reading should be offered at a variety of reading levels. Even in homogeneous classrooms, there will be variation in reading levels.

Some readers read more fluently or faster than others. Text length may become a consideration in student selection as it is more effective if book clubs schedule their reading for approximately the same length of time, with all clubs finishing their reading and meetings on the same date. If a club or two runs over by one meeting or one group ends a few days sooner, those groups will have more or less time to work on after-reading presentations, but generally the schedule operates more efficiently if all clubs can keep to the same basic time frame. One way to achieve this is to offer texts of different lengths. Slow readers are not necessarily weak readers; they may be simply more careful or more reflective readers.

Readers appreciate different styles of writing; consequently, multiple authors may be chosen by the teacher. Some readers gravitate toward novels with more dialogue; some have trouble comprehending novels containing dialect. Other readers may enjoy a novel with more description and elevated language. Even in nonfiction, authors offer divergent styles of writing. However, if classroom lessons during the time the novels will be read are focusing on writer's craft, teachers may wish to choose texts by the same author or authors who write in similar ways.

When choosing books written by several authors, it is also beneficial to choose culturally diverse authors—with "culture" being defined in its broadest terms as ethnicity, race, nationality, religion, gender, geography, and age. In some instances, it would also be beneficial to offer a blend of contemporary and classical writers. Not only will culturally diverse authors offer different perspectives, students may identify with writers who reflect their own cultures while learning from those whom they perceive as coming from different backgrounds and experiences.

Books—fiction and nonfiction alike—are now offered in a range of formats: prose, verse, picture books, and graphic versions, as well as multigenre texts. Some readers prefer one text format, and sometimes readers are looking for opportunities to try a new format. There are also texts that are available in both conventional prose narrative and graphic formats, such as Laurie Halse Anderson's *Speak*, Walter Dean Myers's *Monster*, and Anthony

Horowitz's *Stormbreaker*, as well as many of the classics and some biographies and memoirs such as Marjane Satrapi's *Persepolis: The Story of a Childhood*. Graphic texts are available on many informational topics also.

Book clubs may each read books in a different format, either the same text or a text on the same topic. For example, text clubs may all be reading novels based on Holocaust topics; one club could be reading a prose narrative, one reading a graphic novel, and a third reading a novel written in free verse. Unless lessons were to be focused on literary elements, such as characterization or plot components, one club could elect to read a nonfiction text. A group of English Language Learners (ELL) may be reading a collection of picture books where the pictures support their comprehension of the text. Specific examples for fiction and nonfiction clubs will be shared in later chapters.

Readers do not need to read entire books in book clubs. In circumstances when a teacher may not have three to four weeks to devote to reading, meeting, and presenting a book-length text, students can read short stories for fiction book clubs, memoir essays for narrative nonfiction, and longer articles for nonfiction text clubs. Shorter text reading would not be the appropriate venue for introducing book clubs and teaching the social and discussion lessons associated with book clubs, but short-term text clubs may allow for added experiences in the curriculum.

There are many wonderful collections of short stories written by one author, anthologies of short stories written by a variety of authors, and anthologies that are written by a variety of authors in a variety of formats, such as prose, free verse, poetry, letters, and graphics. In this way, book clubs can read short pieces and either compare authors or compare stories or the information presented in nonfiction pieces within a meeting or two.

For ELL students, the books that a book club is reading may also be available in students' native languages, or if there are multiple students who read in the same language, their book club could employ a book written in their language. As an alternative, a club composed of ELL students may read a few related picture books rather than a full-length novel, as mentioned earlier.

Last, texts can be chosen to offer diverse perspectives on a topic and for diversity in characters, settings, or authors, reflecting the readers or introducing readers to cultures outside their own. It is vital for readers to read texts about and by those with diverse cultural identities—ethnicity, race, nationality, religion, generation, geography, economic status, gender identification, and sexual orientation—to see themselves represented and valued in a book, to encourage empathy and understanding of those they may see as different from themselves, and to become aware of a variety of perspectives in all fields of study.

One of the major advantages of book clubs is that students have choices to read different texts, and the differences, as outlined, can be based on divergent variables.

Considerations for Creating Book Club Groups

There are a few factors to take into consideration when planning book club groups. The two most important are the number of members and the types of learners who will comprise each book club.

One concern is size. Many teachers agree that a group of less than six members is the most effective. It appears that often, with groups of six, four students work and two hold off-task discussions or exhibit off-task behaviors. Five students appears to be an optimal number for book club discussions, especially if there are absentees, which can decrease groups, at times, to four or even three members. In classes with traditionally low absenteeism rates, groups of four would be feasible.

The second customary determination for the composition of collaborative groups is the type of learners. Generally for collaborative projects, learners can be configured heterogeneously by abilities, skills or talents, or multiple intelligence strength; homogeneously, so that each group can be challenged in its own way; self-selected, where students choose their groups; or randomly, using a deck of cards, birthdates, numbering off, or other random determiners.

However, for book clubs, rather than the students forming club membership, the books should guide the composition of the groups. Since the primary goal of text clubs is to read and comprehend a text, it is crucial that readers choose their texts rather than choose their groups (i.e., friends). In many cases, readers will be working with these books for three to four weeks; therefore, group members should be working with texts they *can* read and *will* read, supported by other readers who also are interested in that text. For this to occur, these steps should be followed.

Choosing Texts to Form Text Clubs

Before readers choose their texts, the teacher displays a copy of each book that will be included as text club reading. It can be beneficial to include one more book than the number of clubs. For example, if the class has twenty-five students and there will be five book clubs, there would be at least five choices of books, but six options could be offered in case no students, or only one or two, are interested in one of the selections, as sometimes occurs.

The teacher gives a short book talk about each of the selections, telling the students a little about the plot, setting, characters, and the author. Next, the teacher places one book on each student's desk, in order with Text #1, Text #2, Text #3, and so forth so that one student in every six has a different text and they can pass books five times to examine each text. Texts may be placed on tables at the front of the room for students to come up and peruse, but many times, in that situation, students only examine texts that they think interest them or texts their friends are considering. Placing novels in front of students and inviting them to examine and then pass each individual book ensures that they contemplate each one.

Students are instructed to examine the text in front of them. If the text is a book, they are to look at the front cover and then read the back cover or inside flap, whichever is applicable.

They then are to read one or two pages. The teacher should discuss the importance of reading a few pages, explaining that readers may be interested in the topic or title, be intrigued by any cover art, and be engaged by the synopsis or the excerpt on the cover, particularly since the most engaging part is chosen by the publisher for a blurb; however, the author's writing style may not appeal to them, or some may find the writing or vocabulary too challenging or not challenging enough.

After two or three minutes, the teacher asks students to pass their books to the next student who has a different book (e.g., each student passes to the right or passes to the student behind them) and repeat the process with each book until all students have carefully surveyed all choices (see textbox 2.1 for sample directions for students).

Then the students write down their first, second, and third choices. It is effective to have them write down a reason why they want to read a text, even if only for the first choice. This allows the teacher to recognize reasons that may not be apparent for matching a student with a book and causes the readers to reflect on their choices.

For example, if a student chooses a memoir such as *Soul Surfer* and writes that they surf or have lived near the setting of the book or have a friend who has suffered an injury that affected their life or sports, the teacher realizes that (1) the student has examined the novel and considered the topic, (2) the reader may be more engaged in a novel that has familiar ideas or topics, and/or (3) that the student has some background knowledge that will help with the reading, especially if the text reading level might be considered challenging for that student.

Some students may say they chose a certain book because it only has one main character; others may be familiar with one of the authors; some might cite their reason for preferring a certain nonfiction book because, in that text, the chapters are divided into subsections or there are pictures and illustrations to aid with comprehension.

Discovering and providing a reason for selecting a text to read and discuss also shows that a reader is not choosing texts solely because a friend has chosen it.

Sample Directions for Students

1. I will place a novel in front of you to carefully examine and consider. Look at the front cover and then read the back cover or the inside flaps and one or two pages.
2. When I say, "Pass," pass your book to the student on your right. There will be six passes.
3. After you examine all the choices, write your name on a sheet of paper and list your #1, #2, and #3 choices by title and author.
4. Write a short but good reason for your #1 choice.

Textbox 2.1

The teacher collects the students' choices and divides the students into clubs, giving as many students as possible their top choices. This method allows the teacher to privately determine if students have chosen texts that may be too challenging or not challenging enough as first choices and, if so, to assign their second or third, more appropriate, choice. Having three options also allows the teacher to manipulate the groups, if necessary, providing a chance for teachers to separate students who do not work well together or whose interactions may be detrimental to the group dynamics.

Students who have had prior experiences with book clubs have shared that in the past they chose their group and then the group chose a book. Many have said that they prefer choosing the book in the way outlined here because, in their past experiences, they succumbed to peer pressure to read a book they either did not enjoy or that was not an appropriate reading or interest level for them. Others have said that when they are in groups that are not made up solely of good friends, they notice more diversity of perspectives. In addition, interestingly, some students realize that they are less inclined to admit to their close friends when they don't understand something and need some help, and others have reported that the same students take over leadership roles as they do within their peer group, and therefore this is a chance for others to shine. Perceptive students have noted that new groups offer new opportunities for them to perform in different ways.

In cases where the whole class is reading the same book in "literature or text circles," as defined in chapter 1, students can be grouped by teachers heterogeneously or homogeneously, depending on the goals of the teacher for the students and the text. In some cases, students could select their groups, or the groups could be randomly configured.

When to Include Book Clubs in the Curriculum

In an English/language arts class, it can be effective to employ book clubs as a bridge between the whole-class reading of common texts and independent self-selected reading. The teacher can introduce literature circles two-thirds or three-fourths of the way through a shared novel, after students have learned and practiced reader response journaling and reviewed and applied multiple reading strategies. Teachers can explain the procedures and lessons outlined in the next chapter either during the last chapters of the shared text or by employing the shared text in the model lessons. English/language arts classes can return to book club reading throughout the year with different texts and different book club groupings.

Text clubs can be employed in other disciplines whenever the class would gain from reading multiple texts that present diverse perspectives on the subject being studied in the discipline. Just as important, students will always profit from reading texts written on multiple reading levels or written in a variety of ways or formats or a range of lengths. Teachers may also want to expand a study through the use of a variety of additional texts.

CHAPTER THREE

~

Preparing for Book Clubs

Teaching Social Skills

Students sit in their book clubs, novels and reading journals in front of them. A student nods at another group member. "That was a good question. I agree with the point you made, and I can add another example from the text." In another book club, a student states, "That's an interesting point; I never thought of that. When I read that chapter, I was thinking . . ." In a third group, a student leans forward, makes eye contact, and says, "Jason, I wonder what you thought when you read that," inviting a more reticent group member into the conversation. This is not usual sixth-grade behavior and language, but it is an actual classroom where students have been trained in the social skills necessary for collaborative discussions.

"I tried it once [group project, collaborative presentation, book clubs], and I'll never do that again!" We probably have all heard teachers, especially middle-grade teachers, making this declaration. Teachers place students together in groups, present them with an assignment, and all sorts of behaviors occur, the least of which may be effectively working on the assignment: talking off topic, arguing, refusing to work together, contributions by only a percentage of group members, complaints that other students are not participating or cooperating, and so on. Many teachers quickly give up on the idea of collaboration.

Possibly one of the most important aspects of text clubs is that they can be employed to teach social skills. Like any other proficiency, skills necessary for collaboration have to be modeled and taught. Social skills are not only necessary for successful text club meetings and effective discussions but also the social skills necessary for any collaboration are authentic skills that are becoming more essential as more modern workplaces are reorganizing into collaborative structures.

And, just as important, discussion skills must be explained and demonstrated. If group members do find a way to collaborate, many times this is accomplished with insufficient conversation. The primary social skill necessary for effective collaboration, especially as the guiding component of successful text club meetings, is conversation in which all members participate.

Many English/language arts teachers focus on reading and writing skills and, with the Common Core or the state standards that have replaced them in some states, there has been a push to include teaching such proficiencies across the curriculum in all disciplines. However, many curricula neglect instructing students in speaking and listening skills, standards for which are also included in the Common Core State Standards and individual state standards.

Delineating Social Skills

The most effective way to demonstrate discussion skills, and the social skills that make discussion effective, is to stage a "fishbowl" presentation. The teacher and two other available educators—librarian, other teachers, administrators, aides, or, if necessary, two of the more advanced students— use a short text or poem to generate a literary conversation, or an article to generate a disciplinary conversation, that mimics a book club discussion. The discussion should not be planned or practiced and, indeed, should flow as naturally as possible; the observers need to see that discussion should be a natural response. However, all participants should read the text in advance and bring some notes to the meeting.

While the demonstration is not orchestrated, there may be one exception. One group member can be solicited to abstain from the conversation until another group member invites them to join in, allowing the group to demonstrate that particular common situation and its solution.

The three participants sit in a triangle with the class circled around them as though students are looking into a fishbowl. It may be useful for students to read a copy of the text or view a projected copy of the text that the group will be discussing, although student spectators will be instructed that they are not to concentrate on the content of the discussion at this time; they are to only note the behaviors and "social" comments—*how* they talk—of the participants.

Following the discussion, student spectators are instructed in small groups to brainstorm and write down what they noticed about the conversation and any particular behaviors or nonliterary comments they noted—what the group participants were *doing* and *saying to* each other. Student audience members will notice, "Everyone contributed to the discussion," "It sounded like conversation," and, most important, "Everyone brought up different issues and supported their points with examples from the text."

When class discussions focus on the specifics of the conversation, students will offer observations such as "Everyone took turns." At this point, the teacher should ask, "What does 'taking turns' look or sound like?"

Students will respond with such observations as

- "one person talking at a time"
- "all three people making at least one comment on a topic"
- "no one interrupting"
- "going back and forth among the three group members but not necessarily in any order"

Another student may contribute that "everyone was listening." The teacher should invite reflections on the question "What does *listening* look or sound like?" to elicit such responses as

- "nonspeaking members facing the speaker"
- "making eye contact with the speaker"
- "leaning in toward the speaker"
- "nodding as the speaker makes points"
- "comments such as 'got it'"
- looking in the text to follow the speaker's ideas

Audience members should notice that, in the demonstration, when one of the group members was hesitant to participate, the others invited her to join the conversation; they also should have noted what was said to encourage participation. They could also brainstorm some other ways to show support to the club members, such as "I would love to hear what you think about what I said," or "Can you add anything that you noticed about the character?" or "I remember that you said . . . last meeting. Do you still feel that way about the character?"

Typically at least one student will remark that one person discussed a topic and then, rather than changing the topic, the next speaker builds on the discussion or "talks more about the same topic." The teacher can explain that the concept is referred to as "piggybacking" and invite students to analyze its effectiveness in building a conversation. The class can consider how many comments are usually effective before the efficacy of talking about the same topic expires.

Some other discussion techniques that students note are participants asking questions of each other, participants verifying or confirming each other's comments, and specific ways group members concur and differ with the speaker. It is helpful to ask them to note and reflect on the wording used to concur and, especially, to differ.

A chart can be made and displayed so that group members can practice these behaviors and language in their book club meetings (see figure 3.1).

DISCUSSION TECHNIQUE	WHAT IT LOOKS/SOUNDS LIKE

Figure 3.1.

These are some of the "discussion techniques" that should be included from the class analysis of the sample fishbowl discussion:

- being prepared (reading assigned chapters and bringing the novel and response journal to all meetings)
- listening
- taking turns
- piggybacking on others' ideas
- actively participating
- including all members; encouraging participation
- supporting the ideas of others
- respectful disagreeing
- citing text evidence and examples
- actively participating in the discussion
- asking questions
- anything else students observed or think to add to the list

Designing Discussion Questions

It is essential that during text club meetings students remain on track, discussing the text or topics that derive from or relate to the text, although including personal connections made to the text. This can be achieved in multiple ways. First of all, everyone has to want to read the text, which is achieved by providing a selection of interesting texts and allowing student choice of text, as discussed in chapter 2.

Second, all text club members must have read and interacted with the text prior to each meeting. That can be achieved by requiring readers to maintain reader response journals as they read. Reader response journaling causes readers to interact with the text, provides evidence that they have read and how they have read, and, when brought to meetings, reminds students of what they read and what they found notable about what they read. Reader response strategies and reading journal forms will be discussed in detail in chapter 5.

Third, it is vital that club meetings are built around discussion; therefore, discussion questions are the heart of the book club meeting. However, these are student-led discussions and should be driven by student-designed questions. Each member should be expected to bring one meaningful discussion question to each club meeting, and, therefore, students must learn the characteristics of "good" discussion questions and how to design their own discussion questions.

When asked what makes a good discussion question, students have brain-stormed the following characteristics:

- A good discussion question is based on the text being read.
- A good discussion question is open ended (i.e., does not have a correct answer).
- A good discussion question allows for several credible answers.
- A good discussion question invites multiple perspectives.
- A good discussion question provokes thought before answering.
- A good discussion question makes connections to the text, to the readers' experiences, and/or to the world.
- A good discussion question requires references to the text or is supported by the text.
- A good discussion question generates more questions.
- A good discussion question leads to identifying interesting ideas from the text.
- A good discussion question may require looking back at the text.
- A good discussion question necessitates text analysis.
- A good discussion question leads to a long conversation in which everyone wants to, and is able to, participate.
- A good discussion question goes beyond the book.

After students have brainstormed a list of "good discussion" qualities, they can look at a few sample discussion questions based on a text they have already read or the text presented during the fishbowl discussion and vote on whether the question would generate a meaningful conversation, providing reasons for their response. In triads, students can create one or two discussion questions to test on a neighboring group to determine whether the question generates thoughtful dialogue.

To ascertain the most engaging discussions, students should be advised to create questions based on what they actually want to talk about with their peers, questions that result in discussions concerning what their fellow readers think about a character, event, setting, or issue that interests the questioner. Members should pose questions that are likely to get book clubs talking, not just answering the question, because they are interested in each other's responses. For example, everyone always wants to know what their fellow readers think happened to Jonas at the end of *The Giver*.

Developing a Discussion or Continuing the Conversation

The next social skill lesson centers on developing a discussion. A difficult experience is endeavoring to extend a conversation when everyone agrees with the first answer. But we do not wish one person to answer a question and everyone else to nod or merely say, "I agree." Therefore, classes need to generate ways to concur but still extend the conversation. Some of the language or sentence starters that students have suggested to extend the conversation, building on each other's comments:

- "I agree because . . ."
- "I agree, but I liked the example you gave to support your reasoning. An example I found/thought of was . . ."
- "In the same way, I thought/noticed . . ."
- "I agree, and I would add . . ."
- "I think that is true. In addition . . ."
- "I like that idea but for a different reason, which is . . ."

Teachers also will want to teach students that they do not have to agree with each other but they do need to learn to appreciate each other's answers and to disagree respectfully while continuing the conversation. Some conversation extenders when the responder disagrees with a point made are

- "I can see your point when you said . . .; however, I was thinking . . ."
- "That is a good thought, but did you consider . . .?"
- "I think that may be true; however, I was also thinking . . ."
- "That is a good idea, but another way of looking at it might be . . ."
- "Your point is very interesting. I never thought about it that way. In fact, I was thinking in a completely different direction, which was . . ."
- "I thought that same way until I read further and the character said . . . Does that make you think any differently?"
- "I am not sure I understand your point because . . ."
- "Not only could it mean that, but also it could indicate/suggest/represent . . ."

After a few specific lessons on collaboration social skills and discussion skills, students should be ready to participate in effective, productive book club meetings and presentations as well as other collaborative endeavors.

CHAPTER FOUR

Book Club Procedures and Lessons

Sophia: So why do you think that Kevin put up the blackout poetry with such a mean message about the teacher?

Davon: He says, "I thought people would laugh. People did laugh."

Emma: But why does he want or need people to laugh? Mrs. R's focus lesson today was about character motivation. What was Kevin's motivation?

Julio: I think it was the way he was treated by his family. It says on page 3 that "My ideas are great but he [his older brother Petey] never listens to me." I think he needs the attention because his family doesn't give him any.

Davon: So should we write that down as his character trait "wants attention" and that is his motivation for bullying?

The group all nods.

Teaching through Reading Workshop

Some teachers say, "I would love to have book clubs in my classroom, but I don't have time. I have curriculum to teach. I have to teach reading strategies, literary elements, literary devices, how to compare texts, and so much more to meet standards. I can't give up lesson time!" They don't have to. Book clubs do not preclude teaching language arts; daily focus lessons can go hand-in-hand with book club reading and discussions.

Book clubs can be easily incorporated into a Reading Workshop format in any discipline. For those teachers who may not be familiar with the Reading Workshop format, there are five essential components:

1. the read-aloud;
2. the focus lesson;
3. independent reading and reader response journaling;
4. teacher-student conferring; and
5. student sharing.

It is important for students of any age or grade level to hear text read aloud for a variety of reasons: reading aloud models fluent, expressive reading; readers can learn to appreciate the sound of language; hearing text read aloud expands vocabulary; and listening levels are generally higher than reading levels, and therefore, students can comprehend more complex texts when listening. In a book club unit, the daily read-alouds are the common texts and, as such, build community as students refer back to those texts. The read-aloud can be any short five-minute text, such as a poem, a picture book, a short story, an excerpt, or an article.

Most effectively, the read-aloud can become part of the focus lesson as a mentor text, the text employed as the basis of a teacher think-aloud, which provides a connection to the lesson and to the book club texts and meetings. This is one reason that a long work, such as a novel, is not an effective read-aloud (besides the difficulties that result from student absenteeism). Read-alouds that successfully serve as mentor texts for an individual focus lesson should be chosen intentionally for each lesson.

There is a pattern to teaching and a rationale for teaching certain focus lessons in a particular order or at a particular time; a longer continuing work may not lend itself to a specific focus lesson. As the lesson begins, the teacher reads the selection aloud, having practiced and marked for the most effective rendition, and then introduces the read-aloud as the mentor text for the focus lesson that follows.

The focus lesson is the heart of the Reading Workshop; it is the lesson that is being instructed for the day. Even though teaching should always be derived from the needs of students, most teachers will have a curriculum of lessons to teach and standards to meet in all disciplines, and this can be achieved by means of daily focus lessons. Focus lessons are simple and direct, focusing on one narrow topic, and should last only ten to fifteen minutes, the amount of time students are actually attentive.

The focus lesson always begins with a connection to a past lesson, class conversation, or event that all the students have experienced. The most effective way to impart a focus lesson is through the gradual release of responsibility format, beginning with a teacher model or think-aloud, moving into guided practice in small groups or pairs, and ending as an invitation for independent application. In this case, the instructions for independent application would involve the students applying the lesson to their book club reading or response writing or in their group discussions. Focus lessons can address reading comprehension strategies, reading response strategies, literary elements, text features, author's craft, content material, or disciplinary standards.

Next in Reading Workshop readers spend the next twenty to twenty-five minutes reading their texts independently or, if necessary, pair reading, and five minutes responding in their journals, reflecting on their reading. This is true whether the class is reading a common text, reading texts in small groups such as book clubs, or individually reading self-selected texts. The students are reading independently. During this time, the teacher confers individually with students, getting to know them as readers and supporting them by assessing *if* and *how* they are reading and *what* and *how much* they are comprehending. The teacher encourages reluctant readers, coaches reading strategies, models literate conversation, and discusses disciplinary content in the reading. A portion of this time could also be employed for small-group instruction, especially for students who may have missed a focus lesson or need to repeat a lesson.

While the students are reading or, more typically, after reading, students write a five-minute personal response about what they read, employing during-reading response strategies that have been taught and modeled, scaffolded throughout the year (Roessing, 2009). The purpose of reader response is both reflection on reading and interaction with the text, which increases comprehension. Reader response also allows the teacher to see *what* and *how* readers are reading their texts and *how* and *if* they are interacting with the ideas in the texts. For book clubs, members bring their response journals to meetings, which has the added advantage of reminding them what they read and providing them with conversation topics and ideas.

The last element of Reading Workshop is scheduling five minutes for sharing; readers share something about their reading or a strategy from the focus lesson they implemented during reading. Students can share out to the class or share in pairs or in small groups.

Table 4.1 shows what the Reading Workshop schedule might look like in a typical forty-five-minute or sixty-minute class period.

Table 4.1.

5–10 minutes	Read aloud
10–15 minutes	Focus Lesson (Teacher Model and Guided Practice)
20–25 minutes	Independent reading (independent application of Focus Lesson) and teacher-student conferences and small-group instruction
5 minutes	Reader response journaling
5 minutes	Sharing

Adapting Reading Workshop for Book Clubs

Adaptations to the Reading Workshop format and schedule need to be made for book club reading, meetings, and response formats. It is essential for book clubs to have time to meet and discuss their reading and also have adequate time for reading their texts. Book clubs will be more successful if they meet every other day, rather than every day. This schedule allocates either two nights for students to read the text assigned by the club for the next meeting or reserves every other class period as an independent reading period to be organized in the preceding Reading Workshop format.

On book club meeting days, the Reading Workshop schedule is modified as follows (see table 4.2):

Table 4.2.

5–10 minutes	Read aloud
10–15 minutes	Focus Lesson (Teacher Model and Guided Practice)
20–25 minutes	Book Club Meeting (application of Focus Lesson in discussion)
5 minutes	Book Club Meeting Reflection
5 minutes	Sharing with the other book clubs

Teachers continue to begin with a read-aloud from a text that is somehow related to the book club readings or the discussions to be held, followed by a focus lesson on a reading or discussion strategy, a literary feature, or content information teachers wish club members to discuss in that day's meeting or to think about during their next text reading.

The clubs then meet, following the agenda set out in the following section, hold their discussions, fill out a meeting reflection form where individually they reflect on their meeting and the social skills employed, and, last, share something about their text or their meeting with the rest of the class or with other book clubs.

Book Club Meeting Agenda

The teacher can prepare a meeting agenda so all text club meetings follow the same format and schedule. Here is a sample agenda:

1. After the focus lesson, book club members are to pull your desks into circles (if your desks are not already positioned in small groups).
2. Have your book and your completed reader response journals on your desk.
3. Distribute the reader response sheets submitted to the teacher at the end of the last meeting and add to your reading journals.
4. For the next twenty-five minutes, using texts and notes, discuss your book club's assigned reading following suggestions for supportive, productive discussions (see classroom charts or your notes).
5. Starting with the person who . . . (listen for the day's suggestion), discuss each member's discussion question. You may not cover all questions because some of the questions could elicit so much talk that time runs out.
6. Integrate the current focus lesson into your discussion.
7. When finished with your discussion, make any necessary adjustments to your reading schedule.
8. Collect reader response journals, take to the homework bin, and distribute the meeting reflection forms.
9. Members will *individually* fill out the meeting reflection forms as specifically as possible. Comments will be kept confidential. This will serve as your ticket out the door.
10. Share something from your meeting, for example, a social skill that was implemented well; an insight about your text; or a way you employed the focus lesson in your discussion. Take turns with sharing responsibilities.
11. If there is time, continue reading your text until the end of the period.

A reproducible Book Club Meeting Agenda sample is included in the appendix as figure 4A.1.

After students gather and distribute the response journals that were submitted to the teacher after the last meeting, the teacher will designate the students who are to begin the discussion with their discussion questions, for example, the tallest club member; the member whose birthday is closest to, but preceding, December 31; or the person whose middle name is alphabetically first. It doesn't matter what method of selection the teacher uses; this process prevents students from wasting five to ten minutes debating who will begin.

The designated students share their questions. Students discuss the first question—following the discussion techniques and strategies and practicing the social skills and language charted in chapter 3—and then move on to the next discussion, typically clockwise around the group. The discussion questions serve as a catalyst to conversation, a conversation in which the student who constructed the question also actively participates.

The teacher should make clear that if a resulting discussion leads to other discussion topics related in some way to the text but not necessarily to one of the discussion questions, the goal of the meeting—profound and meaningful discussion about text—is fulfilled. Members should not be concerned about covering all the discussion questions.

In some circumstances, it would be more advantageous to begin the meeting by introducing something that was unclear or confusing to one or more readers when they were reading for the current meeting. In that case, after misinterpretations or confusions are explained or questions answered, the members would initiate conversations based on the prepared discussion questions.

If time allows after the questions are discussed, which is entirely possible when multiple students have created similar questions, club members can comment on the text read based on the focus lesson and also refer to their reader response journals for topics for conversation. Teachers have reported that, using this method, clubs never run out of text conversation in their twenty-five-minute meetings. Reader response journals and meeting reflection forms will be covered in chapter 5.

Before the meetings end for the day, text club members collaboratively choose something to share with the rest of the class. They might select something about or from their texts, a strategy they employed in reading or discussion, or a connection between their text and a recent focus lesson. Club members should take turns sharing.

In some instances, book club members will meet in inter–book club meetings for the five to ten minutes of sharing time. To meet for inter–book club meetings, members of each book club will number off—1, 2, 3, 4, 5. All the 1's will meet as a book club; all the 2's will meet as a book club, and so forth. For their different novels, the inter–book club members compare and contrast aspects covered in the day's focus lesson or designated by the teacher.

Classes that meet for longer than sixty-minute periods have the opportunity to allot time at the end of class for independent reading and response journaling or work on other classwork or lessons, such as vocabulary or writing.

In these ways, book clubs mesh perfectly with Reading Workshop and allow for daily focus lessons on social skills, reading, response writing, literature, and any necessary disciplinary content.

CHAPTER FIVE

~

Book Club Reflections

The students are gathered in their book clubs, ready to begin their meeting. One student distributes the reader response sheets handed in at the end of their last meeting. As they insert them in their reading journals, Ben says, "Oh, Mrs. R wrote a comment on my discussion question. She asked if there were a lot of different opinions in our group about Timothy's decision to take the wallet. There were, weren't there? That was a pretty good discussion. We almost didn't have time to answer other questions and talk about character traits, our focus lesson." Sarah adds, "Yes. Luckily, three of us had that same question because it was so important, so there weren't a lot of questions to discuss that day. I thought it was interesting that you had asked your father his opinion because he is a lawyer."

It is critical for students to be engaged in their own learning. Reflecting on experiences encourages personal understanding, more complex learning, and growth. We want students to learn to connect events and knowledge and construct meaning from their classroom experiences and work—in this case, their book club meetings and readings, resulting in analysis of those experiences and application to future learning and academic practices. Students should learn to reflect in order to make sense of learning and to modify their behaviors and enhance learning and to gain insight into themselves as learners.

There is a dual purpose of book clubs. The first is to educate students to work collaboratively within a small group to accomplish specified goals. The second objective—reading, comprehending, and synthesizing a text—should result more effectively from successful collaboration. Students need to be trained to reflect on these undertakings, together with all the strategies, skills, and experiences connected to those two endeavors so that reflection becomes ingrained and habitual.

Book Club Meeting Reflections

Collaborating and participating actively and productively in small groups is a primary behavior necessary for the contemporary workplace and, therefore, is a real-life skill. Setting goals and working successfully toward those goals occurs within group work through communication. As the social skills involved in collaboration are modeled and taught, group members individually need to observe and monitor their individual progress, discerning what skills they are employing beneficially and what competences they still need to develop.

By reviewing the conversations, activities, and learning during their current meetings, participants also can analyze the efficacy of group communication skills in achieving the outcomes of comprehending and synthesizing the text.

To promote an expectation of and atmosphere for reflection, teachers need to designate time for individual reflection and for book club and self-evaluation for students to learn from their experiences during that meeting. On the agenda presented in chapter 4, a five-minute period is allotted for individual meeting reflection after the meeting has concluded and each book club has shared with the class.

To guide students through the process of thoughtful reflection, a meeting reflection form is distributed and constitutes each student's "ticket out the door" at the end of class. A reproducible Book Club Meeting Reflection Form sample is included in the appendix as figure 5A.1. A fifth-grade student's completed meeting reflection form is shown here in figure 5.1.

When students become comfortable with collecting the information necessary for reflection, teachers can teach them to evaluate their growth and that of their group and write a short reflection, processing their observations. Beginning with a form should scaffold students into more reflective thinking and writing about their experiences and learnings; after a few rehearsals with the form, students should be able to reflect on, and write about, the skills employed in meeting discussions.

This was our fourth meeting. We seemed to be having some really good conversations. Everyone brought a discussion question to the meeting, and the questions were better than they had been; we talked more about each question than we had before. Everyone was caught up in their reading and had something to say. We talked about

---

TEXT CLUB MEETING REFLECTION (Write neatly)

Name Lauren   Text Title *Amal Unbound,* Chapters 1-10

The Meeting – Discussing the Text

Today we discussed why Amal's parents were upset about having a baby girl and why Amal's parents would want to keep her away from her best friend Omar.

From our discussion I learned why Amal's mother went into a depression after having a baby girl and how the hormones just make it worse.

An interesting point made was Amal's parents only kept her away from her friend Omar because they wanted to protect her because it was an inappropriate relationship with a servant's son.

A question I still have about the text — or — What I want to find out now is that at the beginning of the novel Amal wants to be a teacher. What will change as the plot continues? Will she be able to become a teacher? Will she still want to?

The Meeting – Social Skills

I felt that the meeting went well   because we all had something to contribute and/or share. We all had different points of view and ideas that were intersting to hear and add to. I added on to Alana's idea that Amal's parents were keeping her from her best friend because they wanted to protect her. Eliza kept eye contact whenever anyone was talking. No one fidgeted and everyone seemed deeply interested in what everyone else had to say.

+ **What I did well today**	— **What I need to work on**	= **What I tried**
+ being prepared + listening	+ actively paticipating	+ supporting others
= respectful disagreeing — agreeing and extending	= piggybacking on other ideas	
= turn-taking + including all group members	= making eye contact with speakers	

Figure 5.1.

the decisions that the characters made and how they impacted each other. Everyone took turns, which had been a problem in our group. I am still working on eye contact and think I am remembering to look at the person who is speaking and this meeting I even nodded a few times when I agreed. Before, I was always looking at my paper for something to say next. I think we still need to work on "coming to a consensus," our most recent skill focus lesson.

Reading Reflection: Reader Response Journals

Research shows the importance of reader response writing. The 2000 report of the National Reading Panel states, "Teaching students to use . . .writing to organize their ideas about what they are reading is a proven procedure that enhances comprehension of the text." *Writing to Read: Evidence for How Writing Can Improve Reading*, a report commissioned by the Carnegie Corporation, listed that the number one core instructional practice effective in improving student reading is to "have students write about the texts they read" (Graham and Hebert, 2010). Reader response compels readers to interact with the text and makes visible for readers and their teachers the depth of text comprehension.

Reading response writings are short, spontaneous, informal, and personal to the reader and should not disrupt or sabotage enjoyment of reading. Effective written responses should be meaningful and induce readers to explore, question, and challenge text and make connections and inferences so they can construct meaning and learn from text.

The goals of reader response journaling are twofold. Responses let teachers "see" readers' thinking to discern *what* they read and *how* they read. Journal entries allow teachers to evaluate individual comprehension and, as a tool for formative assessment, determine what reading strategies they need to teach and to whom they need to teach those strategies. It allows them to perceive what readers understood and what they did not and even, in many cases, exactly what caused misunderstandings.

The second reason to employ reader response journals is that it causes readers to read more closely and critically for increased comprehension. Many proficient readers read too quickly for maximum comprehension; reading with reflection in mind causes them to slow down. Teachers can use journals to encourage students to think more critically by writing comments or questions next to journal entries that provoke deeper thinking or prompt wider thinking.

In text club reading and meetings, response takes on an additional purpose. The simple act of writing about what they read increases comprehension. However, when club members bring their completed response journals to their meetings, their discussion question and their personal response to that question have been recorded, demonstrating that they have not only designed a question but also considered answers to that question, rendering themselves a contributor to the discussion. In addition, the response journals will contain at least three reflections on the reading for that meeting, providing the responder with notes for discussion and the group with plenty of topics to contemplate. Written responses assist the reticent members and the forgetful students in contributing to the conversation. For those students, their journals are a resource and a support.

If readers are not familiar with reader response strategies, teachers can guide them to stop reading after around twenty to twenty-five minutes and write a five-minute reflection on what they are thinking about what they read. As shown in table 4.1 from chapter 4, this time is built into the Reading Workshop schedule. Like any other strategy, response should be modeled, practiced, and scaffolded. As a focus lesson, the teacher can read aloud a short text or the beginning of a text, possibly a text related to the upcoming book club readings, and model a five-minute response as a think-aloud. The class can then read another short text or continue with the text the teacher began reading aloud and write their own five-minute responses.

Each student's response will be different. Some will have written more in five minutes; others will write shorter responses. Some responses will be more profound than others. As students and their proficiencies vary, so will their responses. This is true differentiation.

When learning to respond to text, many students will simply write summaries, or in some cases, they were trained that summarizing *is* response. Teachers will want more effective responses that demonstrate interaction with text, such as activating prior knowledge; asking questions; making connections, inferences, and predictions; determining important details; visualizing; and applying "fix-up" strategies, such as noticing vocabulary and thinking about text features, to monitor and increase comprehension; these are all effective reading strategies. Summarizing is a good strategy, especially for remembering what was read and for learning to discriminate when choosing important details. Another method employed to encourage readers to write response or reflection, rather than summary, is to introduce response starters (Roessing, 2009) and model responses to text.

A two-sided journal form, which includes both strategies discussed above, is an effective way to begin journaling for students who are learning response writing. On the front page of the journal, students bullet important events from the novel, highlighting new characters. There are multiple purposes for this. The summary helps them practice determining important details, an important strategy for summarizing, because the form has a limited number of lines. In their meetings, students can consider what events each found significant to write down; this helps the less proficient students discern the type of details that may be important.

The bullet points also remind readers of the plot events and the order in which they happened for meeting discussion. If any students wish to read ahead, they list the events only from the next meeting's assigned chapters, using another form for the future chapters. During discussion, they can refer back to the events of the chapters that are the focus of the meeting so they know what *not* to mention or reveal during the meeting.

The form also provides a place for readers to write their discussion questions, ensuring they have prepared good questions for the meeting and ascertaining that the teacher will see the original questions being generated for the meetings and being discussed during the meetings.

For the responses on the back of the journal, readers are advised to stop three times while reading and, using the response starters to track their thoughts, write short personal reflections about what they just read.

The teacher will introduce the journal as a Reading Workshop focus lesson. Based on the first part of the day's read-aloud, the teacher will model a summary of events for the first page, a sample discussion question, and one response for the second page beginning with one of the response starters listed, thinking aloud while completing those tasks. As the guided practice, students can add a few more events, a discussion question, and a practice response based on the last part of the read-aloud. A reproducible basic two-sided book club journal for teaching and practicing response is included in the appendix as figures 5A.2 and 5A.3, titled Book Club Basic Journal, pages 1 and 2.

For students who are familiar with, or when they become familiar with, writing reflective responses to text, teachers can progress to double-entry journals, again modeling and guiding students as they practice of this type of response. A double-entry journal, also known as a dialectical journal, is basically a T-chart. For the left column, readers choose something that they find thought-provoking or notable from the text—a sentence, a phrase, a quote, a fact, a term, a new word, or in a novel, a character, a setting, or a plot element. In the right column, readers record their personal responses—questions, inferences, insights, connections, predictions, evaluations, reflections—to the text. This works as well for fiction and nonfiction texts, in both English/language arts and disciplinary classes.

If students are resistant to stopping and writing in their journals *during* reading, they may be more comfortable using sticky notes directly on the text *as* they read. They can then transfer those notes to the left column and respond to them in the right column.

An advantage of the double-entry journal is that teachers can see and readers can remember exactly to what they were responding and, in discussions, refer to text in their comments. This also prepares students for writing essays and for standardized reading test responses where they are expected to cite evidence from text.

The teacher can design a very basic form to begin double-entry journaling; a reproducible form is included in the appendix as figure 5A.4, Book Club Basic Double-Entry Journal.

Figure 5.2 is an example of a double-entry journal based on chapter 7 of the novel Mr. Popper's Penguins, combining responses from two readers.

Name _____	Text Title _Mr. Popper's Penguins_
My Notes for Our Next Text Club Meeting Chapter 7	
Something I noticed in the novel (page #) (a character, something about the setting, an event, a decision, a quote from the text)	What I am thinking about that… (inferences, connections, reflections)
"Captain Cook Builds a Nest" (p.44)	This makes me think that maybe C.C. moves out of the house and build a nest in the yard _because_ nests are usually outdoors and penguins usually live outdoors. Maybe he can't get used to being in a house.
"Mrs. Popper was…rather belatedly doing the breakfast dishes." (p.44) "Mrs. Popper had not get gotten around to straightening the house" (p.45) "Mrs Popper laughed…as they saw the results of CC's trips through the house." (p 47)	I am thinking that, since Captain Cook came, Mrs. Popper is not as worried about neatness in the house; therefore, I was not really surprised that she laughed instead of getting upset at all the things Captain Cook put in the icebox.
the rookery (p. 48)	I infer that a rookery is a nest _because_ Mr. Popper then says "he couldn't find any stones to build his nest with."
Mr. Popper dressed "like a penguin" (p. 49)	I do not understand why Mr. Popper would want to dress like the penguin since most people do not dress like their pets, but now he is much neater and better dressed and groomed than he usually is.
clothesline (p. 49)	I predict that Mr. Popper is going to use the clothesline to make a leash to take Captain Cook for a walk and that Captain Cook will try to pick up things outside. Maybe he will find rocks for his nest. I am thinking that he might try to take things from the neighbor's yard.

A discussion question—one that will generate conversation and encourage different opinions/points of view:

How is Captain Cook changing the Poppers' lives and do these type of situations happen when families adopt pets or only with unusual pets?

My answer to my question:

_____
_____
_____
_____

Figure 5.2.

Assigning readers "roles"—discussion leader, illustrator, character critic, quote monger, vocabulary finder, for example—as many teachers facilitating book clubs have done in the past, can lead readers to read merely for the purpose of their jobs or until their jobs, such as "three new or interesting vocabulary words," are completed or to employ narrow reading strategies, for instance, if they are the illustrator for the meeting, simply visualization. Readers with an assigned "role" appear to employ little analytical thinking about what they read. Assigning meeting roles also presents a problem when members holding significant discussion positions, such as the discussion leaders, are absent.

Therefore, completing a response journal can benefit students as they read more strategically and discuss more thoroughly, even when multiple members of the group are missing. Teachers will most likely observe a correlation between the use of a response sheet with a variety of reflections and active, extended discussion.

However, as valuable as the response journals can be to contributing to the club discussion, there is no requirement to include those responses as part of the meeting conversation. The purpose of response journals is not to have students merely read their responses to their group but also to suggest topics if the group has run out of discussion topics or to support those students who are reluctant to take charge of the conversation; their journals provide them with something to add to the conversation. Conversation during meetings can be so productive and comprehensive that participants may find themselves not even referring to their sheets. The effort of actively reflecting while reading can carry over into the meeting; one simple statement can engender a multifaceted conversation.

As students become comfortable composing double-entry responses, teachers can create more complex response journals that elicit critical thinking and employ multiple reading strategies to produce deep conversations in text club meetings. These double-entry response journals are particularly effective for text club discussions about literary elements. A reproducible double-sided form is included in the appendix as figures 5A.5 and 5A.6, Book Club Advanced Double-Entry Journal, pages 1 and 2.

The second page of the double-entry journal can be adapted to include a variety of prompts for different curricula taught during book club units. For example, if the Reading Workshop focus lesson centers on character traits and a character's decisions and motivations, a double-entry journal can be customized to guide readers to reflect on those particular elements as in figure 5A.7, Book Club Double-Entry Character Journal, page 2, in the appendix.

Yet another version of the double-entry journal's second page encompasses the types of information provided by students in the previously assigned roles but requires that all club members provide a discussion question, a quote, and a vocabulary word, as well as a question, inference, or prediction. Therefore, if any member is absent the remaining members can still hold a thorough discussion of the text, and, more important, all readers are employing all reading strategies and considering multiple aspects of the text. Figure 5.3 is an example written in response to the poem "Casey at the Bat,"

Based on reading the poem "Casey at the Bat" by Ernest Lawrence Thayer	
From the Text:	My Thoughtful Reflection:
1.Discussion Question or Point:	What I Am Thinking About That
Next time Mudville has a game, do you think Casey will be as cocky and let strikes go by?	There really is no hint in the poem about his future behavior, but he seems to like to control the crowd ("Casey raised his hand") and he is proud ("Pride in Casey's bearing"), so I think he will hit the first one but try to make it a HR.
2. Quote or Main Character & Traits	What I Am Thinking About That
"Oh, **somewhere** in this favored land the sun is shining bright, The band is playing somewhere, and **somewhere** hearts are light; And **somewhere** men are laughing, and **somewhere** children shout,"	From the repetition of "somewhere" I could infer that he struck out because it led me to think that **somewhere** ELSE these things were happening, but not in Mudville
3. Vocabulary/Interesting Word, Definition, and Sentence it appeared in	What I Am Thinking About That
fraud - wrongful deception intended to result in financial or personal gain. "Fraud!" cried the maddened thousands, and echo answered, "Fraud!"	I don't think that the crowd really thought that the refree was deceptive or getting any personal gain from the call, but I do think they wanted to believe that he was wrong because they couldn't believe Casey would make a mistake like that.
4. A Question, Inference, or Prediction	What I Am Thinking About That
My inference: Flynn and Blake were not strong baseball players	Based on 1) the terms "hoo-doo" and "cake" 2) People **thinking**, "if only Casey could but get a whack at that," assuming that Flynn and Blake will strike out before Casey gets his turn at bat. 3) "Flynn let drive a single, to the **wonderment** of all."

Figure 5.3.

and a reproducible form is included in the appendix as figure 5A.8, Book Club Double-Entry Varied Topics Journal, page 2.

Similarly, if the class lesson focuses on disciplinary content, the journal can be customized to direct readers' reflections to those concepts in their texts. For example, in text clubs centered on a study of the events of 9/11, the left column could contain such topics for "From the Text" prompts as "9/11-Related Events," "How Character(s) Was/Were Affected by Events," "Character's Reactions," and so forth. For informational texts, prompts can focus on details encountered or learned.

Response journaling results in readers interacting with text and thinking more deeply about the text as they read. After reading, response writing provides and facilitates text club meeting conversation. When journal pages are collected at the end of each meeting, they provide teachers with assessment of each student's reading, thinking, and preparation for that meeting. Journals enable teachers to monitor individual comprehension and to keep current with club discussions. If students are absent for any text club meetings, they remain responsible for maintaining and handing in their response journals. Additionally, journals can serve as a basis for points or grades for the Text Club unit as discussed in chapter 7 on assessment.

Paired with meeting reflections, text club members will think critically about their reading and the discussions developing from those readings, resulting in more multifaceted learning and growth as a learner.

CHAPTER SIX

~

Book Club
Text Synthesis and Presentations

Five students stand in the front of the classroom, a large decorated bag in front of each. As the first student pulls an item from the bag, the audience, composed of members of the four other class book clubs, leans forward in anticipation. Maria sets a book on the table in front of the bag. "After the family settles in their house in Maine, they visit their neighbor Mrs. Falala and bring her books." She reaches into the bag again and takes out a toy cow. "Reena's mother volunteers her and her younger brother Luke to take care of the neighbor's cow, Zora. The neighbor, also has . . . (she brings out another toy and two stuffed animals) a pig, a cat, and a snake!" (Creech, 2016)

Chapter 5 addressed response written *during* the reading of a text. The objectives of during-reading response for the reader are interactive reading, increased comprehension, and critical thinking, as well as providing a method of taking "notes" in preparation for meeting discussions. The advantage of reader response journals for the teacher is the ability to assess the reading and comprehension of individual readers, a type of one-to-one virtual conference.

Equally important for comprehension and learning is after-reading response, response that takes readers back to the text for synthesis and increased long-term learning. In book clubs, post-reading response can serve another purpose—sharing the text read with the other book clubs and, potentially, other audiences. When the book clubs finish reading and discussing their books, each club is required to collaborate on a book presentation of their choice. Preparing these presentations serves as after-reading reflection.

41

Sharing their texts with other readers in this way also introduces other students to books they may want to read independently.

Effective after-reading response employs a text reformulation or "text rewrite" strategy. Readers reconstruct the books read into another type of text, melding the text with what they learned through the text. This synthesis, a critical-thinking skill that involves putting together assorted parts to make a new whole, helps readers in all disciplines not only to relate information learned through the reading of a text and the club discussions but also to rethink the meaning of this learning and connect it to other learning, enhancing their developing views of the world.

There are numerous methods for text clubs to share their books with their classmates and beyond. In keeping with the goal of teaching collaboration skills, the presentations should be designed as a cooperative endeavor.

The components of an effective collaborative project include reading, writing, speaking, and listening. Most essential is that this type of project includes both elements of independence, where each student is responsible for his or her own portion of the presentation or job within the presentation, and elements of interdependence, wherein the students and their individual parts work together. In that way, the old adage "the whole is greater than the sum of its parts" becomes true. Successful collaborative projects also value diversity, individual skills, multiple intelligences, and the academic/intellectual, artistic/creative, affective/social, and technical talents of group members.

The most significant factor is that presenters share their books in a way that makes sense to those who have not read this book. The teacher should remind presenters that the audience has not read the book; therefore, book club members should first storyboard their books or examine their response journals summaries and select the most central or essential events, ensuring those are included in the presentation. A rubric for the presentation will include a requirement to incorporate all plot elements—inciting incident, conflict, climax, resolution—as well as the setting(s) and all the major characters. A sample rubric is included at the end of this chapter.

There are a variety of ways to present books to an audience of potential readers and even the community at large. A few examples of the more successful presentations have been to prepare and recite I Am poetry, present book bag projects, stage skits or puppet shows, narrate book summaries accompanied by visuals and other media enhancements, or videotape a modified form of multimodal book trailers. It is more effective if book clubs choose their methods of presentation—choice generates increased motivation and engagement—or design their own presentation mode, but if the teachers wish to ensure a variety of presentations, book clubs could sign up for one, first come-first served, or choose a presentation method out of a bowl.

I Am Poetry

The traditional I Am format is composed of three stanzas, each line beginning with "I" plus a verb, beginning and ending with "I am." The traditional format is depicted in textbox 6.1, but students should be encouraged to substitute more appropriate verbs if necessary.

I am . . .	I pretend . . .	I understand . . .
I wonder . . .	I feel . . .	I say . . .
I hear . . .	I touch . . .	I dream . . .
I see . . .	I worry . . .	I try . . .
I want . . .	I cry . . .	I hope . . .
I am . . .	I am . . .	I am . . .

Textbox 6.1.

Presenting their book through I Am poetry is effective for students who work better individually because they can each write their own poem. The book club members each choose a character from their book, ascertaining that all the major characters are included, and compose an I Am poem as that character. When creating an I Am poem, the format compels the reader to identify and understand that character's perspective on events and relationships and requires students to read more critically as they re-explore the text, and the events and decisions within the text, from a particular point of view. This activity encourages, and trains, readers to read and interpret from multiple perspectives and, hopefully, becomes a strategy they will apply to future reading.

The format also causes readers to contemplate how events and the other characters may have influenced and affected a character. As students write the lines for their characters, they are obliged to reflect on what the particular character would *wonder, pretend, dream,* and so on—even if not explicitly mentioned in the novel—and analyze the reasons. This is critical thinking.

The next step would be for the group to meet, share their poems, and check their storyboard or novel summary to ensure that all major events have been incorporated into at least one of the character's poems.

The next step would be to plan their presentation as a performance, perhaps incorporating choral techniques and/or choreography or staging. Each member could read his or her entire poem, collaboratively designing the most effective order of appearance, or each member could read the line that begins with the same verb. There are countless permutations; the book club determines the most advantageous design. Choral techniques, such as varying volume, tempo, tone, and pitch; cumulative reading; echoing; antiphonal responses; or reading in a line-around fashion can enhance the performance as would choreographing how the presenters stand and move.

A group read *Just a Drop of Water* by Kerry O'Malley Cerra in their book club. The students decided to present their novel through I Am poetry. Club members wrote and presented poems as the main character, Jake Green; his best friend, Sameed; the school bully, Bobby; Sam's sister, Amber; and Jake's father. A third-grade group read and discussed *Because of Winn-Dixie*, writing and performing poetry as Opal, the Preacher, Gloria Dump, Miss Franny, Otis, and, of course, Winn-Dixie. In another class, a small group read Linda Sue Parks's novel *A Long Walk to Water*. The creative triad presented as the two main characters, Salva, a Sudanese Lost Boy in 1985, and Nya from 2008 . . . and as Water.

Figure 6.1 shows the poems of three of the characters from K. A. Holt's *Rhyme Schemer* and the creative way the presenters arranged the performance of their stanzas.

Plot or Character Book Bag Presentations

Another more individually prepared presentation is the book bag presentation. This presentation style appears to intrigue the audience of classmates the most with its element of surprise, as demonstrated in the opening scenario of this chapter.

In this presentation, the book club members may divide the book by chapters, each taking an equal percentage of the book. Each member places in a bag of objects that represent the characters, setting, and plot elements of those chapters, retelling the story as they pull objects out of the bag. For example, for chapter 1 of Jennifer Richard Jacobson's middle-grade novel *The Dollar Kids*, the book club member might fill the bag with

- a comic to represent the passion of main character Lowen—drawing comics,
- a bag of Twizzlers, representing Lowen sending Abe to the store where Abe was killed in a random shooting,

I am Kevin, a middle grade bully.
I wonder why I have to ride to school with Petey, my brother.
I see all the kids I can make fun of, like Freckle-Face Kelly.
I hear Petey saying *Get out* and Mrs. Smithson telling me to *Get out.*
I want to find my notebook that Petey threw out the car window.

I am Robin, a boy who wants to be noticed.
I wonder why Kevin hates me so.
I hear Kevin calling me "short." I'm not that short.
I see a poetry notebook lying on the sidewalk.
I want to give it back to Kevin. But, no, I will get my revenge!

I am Mrs. Little, the school media specialist.
I wonder if Kevin realizes how creative he is.
I hear the fighting, the name-calling, and tears.
I see this talented poet defacing the library books.
I want to help Kevin see that he can use his talent for good.

I am Kevin, so mad it was Shorty Robin who found my notebook.
I pretend that I am like a stone.
I feel – I don't feel; I am a stone.
I touch and punch Robin as he sits on top of me, hitting me.
I worry that I will be suspended from school.
I cry out by writing blackout poems using pages from books.

I am Robin, a boy on a mission.
I pretend that I am the poetry bandit.
I feel that I am now in control; Kevin is scared of me.
I touch the poetry notebook… Oh, what I can do with this!
I worry that my secret will be discovered.
I cry when I am slammed under the sink.

I am Mrs. Little, a quiet angel watching on Kevin's shoulder.
I pretend to be indifferent as I watch Kevin shelve books.
I feel like he needs someone to care and notice him.
I touch the pages of classic books he marked with poems.
I worry Kevin needs to find peace and feel important—to find where he fits.
I plant a flyer for a poetry Open Mic night.

I am Kevin, who shelves books in the library with for detention.
I understand now what it's like to be bullied.
I say I don't want to go to the family dinner, but to Open Mic night with Mrs. Little.
I dream Kelly's freckles are stars and galaxies.
I try to make up with Robin.
I hope Petey's band like my rhymes for their songs.
I am a middle school poet.

I am Robin, a boy that has the power…. I am untouchable.
I understand that I am doing the same thing as Kevin, but I don't care.
I say "Poetry Boy! Poetry Boy!"
I dream that I will be known as the poetry bandit.
I try to make Kevin ghost-write for me.
I hope that someone will see me.
I too am a lost boy, trying to get some attention.

I am Mrs. Little, the one advocate Kevin has at school.
I understand Kevin's family might not see how special he is.
I show up at the most important times to point out Kevin's talent to his parents, rescue him
        from a family dinner night gone bad, and help to find peace with a classroom brawl.
I try to be a superhero to fly in and make Kevin's world right.
I hope he will notice the bound book of his poems I cataloged and added to the school collection.
I will keep an eye on him and help him along, inviting him to another poetry night.
I am a life changer, lurking in the shelves of Kevin's life.

Figure 6.1.

- a map of Cornwall, England, or a baking tray to symbolize Lowen's mother's heritage or profession,
- a stethoscope signifying Lowen's father's dream to bring medical care to an underserved community,
- a phone to represent the phone call advising the Grover family that their application for a dollar house in Millville was accepted, and/or
- a lottery ticket to signify they were entered in a lottery for one of the five dollar houses.

Students will usually cover more than one chapter and, typically, there may be one to two objects representing events and characters in each chapter; but, as in this case, the first chapter can establish the story line and introduce many of the characters.

As the students pull out the objects from their bags, they retell the story. The bag can also become part of the story. Students could possibly decorate the bag with a key scene from those chapters or as an object. Mrs. Luella Bates Washington Jones's large purse in the short story "Thank You, Ma'am" would be a good choice for the teacher to model a book bag, or story bag, presentation.

Another way the club could divide the presentation is by characters. Each reader would choose a character and fashion a bag of objects important to that character. The club could then decide whether to tell the story character by character or by chapters, using a narrator to tell the main events and different characters chiming in during each chapter in which they were involved.

While each member is responsible for his or her own bag and individually prepares their presentation of the objects in that bag, the group collaboratively checks their storyboard or novel summary to ensure all key events are covered in the collective presentation. Synthesis occurs as the readers evaluate what item would be important to, or representative of, each event or to each character. Audience members watch expectantly as objects are pulled out of each bag. In this way, the presentation offers an element of surprise.

Skits or Puppet Shows

Kids like to act—or at least many do. When readers turn their novel into a skit, they need to act out four key scenes: the exposition that introduces the background of the story—setting, major characters, and the protagonist's goal; the inciting incident that initiates the conflict; the climax or protagonist's decision that provides a turning point; and the resolution. The skit should also include a narrator who connects the four scenes; otherwise, it will consist of disparate events, and since the audience is not familiar with the story, they will not understand the presentation. The characters should be introduced or display large name tags or nameplates.

Since costumes and scenery may be difficult to create, a puppet show can achieve the same purpose as a skit. Students can use a box, with a slit across the back of the top for scenery and a rectangular cutout in the middle of the topside for puppets attached to rulers or dowels to be lowered in front of the scenery. Bankers' boxes, turned on their sides, work very well, providing a stage area that will be approximately eleven inches high and fifteen inches wide. The presentation requirements are the same as those for skits: exposition, inciting incident, conflict, climax, and resolution, together with narration to connect the scenes.

In one class, the book club members read a mystery and were reluctant to relate the resolution and ruin the book for future readers, but they wanted to present a skit. They followed the guidelines and solved the problem by presenting two possible resolutions and inviting the audience to read the book to discover which ending was the correct outcome of the mystery. When given a choice of presentation projects, students will use their creativity to make their selection work.

Multimedia Retellings

For this type of presentation, book club members prepare a narrated summary of the novel, accompanied by a video or PowerPoint–type presentation of images and possibly appropriate music. Book club members can create the pictures, or they can obtain and scan or download images that represent the characters, settings, and events. Designing a musical background arrangement that corresponds to the topic or the mood of the novel or that enhances the narration of each scene involves critical thinking and technology skills as students think through music they already know or search for music new to them. They are now thinking in multimedia design and recognizing the relative effectiveness of presenting in this format.

Book Trailers or Movies

Book trailers are video advertisements designed to interest readers in a book, much as a movie trailer is designed to promote a movie to prospective viewers. While a typical book trailer is only a few minutes long and does not reveal much of the plot, as an after-reading presentation, students are asked to reveal more plot elements, as they are in a skit presentation, although the technique can be less of a retelling and more highlighting, with voice-overs, the interesting or dramatic aspects of each plot element: the characters, setting, problem, climax, and solution. The differences between a trailer and a skit are that there need not be narration to connect the scenes into a story and a trailer has more of a mood of suspense.

After viewing and analyzing professional book trailers or movie trailers, book club students collaboratively create the trailers for their books using digital media such as iMovie or cameras, audio recording materials, and editing software. They can act scenes or use still or moving images and text, making artistic design decisions such as color, graphics, font size and type, and transitions. They can add music to enhance the video. One advantage to this presentation mode is that book trailers help students develop important "new literacies" skills as they adapt mono-modal print texts into multimodal compositions.

Student-Generated Presentation Formats

There are alternatives that students may suggest or design, and typically students will put more time, effort, and enthusiasm into these self-generated projects because they are more meaningful to and expressive of the creators. Students have staged interview shows with hosts asking questions of character guests; news broadcasts with reporters reporting on plot events and interviewing characters; and short legal trials based on the events in a novel. One group who read *The War between the Classes* involved the audience in some of the activities in which the characters in the novel participated as they summarized the plot. As long as book club members are able to relate the story and adhere to the rubric (see the rubric discussion at the end of this chapter), their presentation will be successful and fulfill the dual objectives of the assignment: to serve as an effective after-reading synthesis and as an introduction to the book to the other students and potential readers of the novel.

The Advantages of Presentations

Besides reviewing the text read and discussing its meaning in more depth when choosing and planning one of these presentations, all the advantages of collaboration inherent in the common goal of designing, developing, staging, and presenting a project together are integral to this undertaking.

Another significant benefit is the act of preparing and performing for an authentic audience. Students are presenting their books to the other students in their class, grade, or school to share books that the audience may not have read and to demonstrate their learning through the book. Other audiences—students in other schools, parents, and community members—can be reached through a variety of media, adding to students' technology skills. Students can videotape presentations to be employed as future models or, archived as part of the classroom or school library, as information for future students who may be seeking a book to read.

In many of these presentations, students not only map storyboards for their novels but also are writing in other genres, such as scripts or poetry. Employing other skills, they choreograph their recitations and movement, assuming roles as directors and actors. Additionally they may serve as set and/ or costume designers and music supervisors or score composers to bring the scenes to life or enhance digital presentations.

According to *Forbes*, more than one-third of business managers surveyed found their recently matriculated hires to be deficient in public speaking skills. They are not referring to only the delivery of speeches and public talks but, more often, professional presentations—speaking in front of small groups. It is clear that schools need to teach public speaking skills and strategies and compel students to practice speaking skills more often and in more circumstances to develop confident, fluent speakers. In addition, listening and speaking standards are included in the Common Core State Standards as well as in many states who have created their own standards.

Teacher Model Lessons

Before students choose a presentation style or format, teachers need to share exemplars for students to analyze and deconstruct, noting elements that were particularly effective and interesting. Multiple sample projects based on one short story is the most effective way. As one lesson, the teacher and students could read a short story together and then hold a short discussion as if they were participating in a book club meeting. They could then storyboard the text—summarizing the plot into approximately ten to twelve events, highlighting the main characters, and dividing the story into "scenes." In the following, all the examples are based on the Langston Hughes short story "Thank You, Ma'am," but any story appropriate for the class can be employed.

In "Thank You, Ma'am," the main characters—in fact, the only characters—are an adolescent named Roger and a lady named Mrs. Luella Bates

Washington Jones. For this text, the teacher would demonstrate writing and presenting an I Am poem as Roger or as Mrs. Luella Bates Washington Jones.

Another teacher model would be a Plot or character bag presentation. Examples of objects exhibited could stem from the first scene of the story where Roger, dressed in *tennis shoes* and *blue jeans*, tries to snatch Mrs. Jones's *large purse* at eleven o'clock at night (*clock*). After the force of her broken purse strap knocks him to the ground, she tells him that his face is dirty (*a washcloth*).

To model a character bag, the teacher could introduce objects from Mrs. Jones's bag, using a large purse as the actual bag holding the items to be presented; some of these objects could include a *five-pound weight* representing her strength, a *key* to her room in a boarding house, a *small door* signifying leaving her door open, the *wallet* as a object to symbolize her trust in Roger, *lima beans* and a package of *cocoa* from the dinner Mrs. Jones shared with Roger, a *brush* or a *curling iron* as representative of her job at a beauty parlor, and the *$10 bill* she gave Roger. As a guided practice in pairs, the class could list the objects that would be presented from Roger's bag.

The teacher could work with two students to present a sample scene for a skit based on the story by staging the inciting incident scene from the story when Roger tries to grab Mrs. Luella Bates Washington Jones's purse and falls, and she picks him up. They should also demonstrate the narrations leading to the scene and connecting it with the next scene.

As an example for a multimedia book summary, the teacher could reveal the images she might choose as she retells the story and ask students to suggest appropriate music that might accompany the retelling. An obvious choice of music to accompany narration of and images for "Thank You, Ma'am" is Carl Perkins's "Blue Suede Shoes," as well as songs about stealing and songs about helping others.

Demonstrating a book trailer presentation, teachers can design and show actual trailers they created for the story; there are also trailers available on YouTube that students could critique, comparing live acting to static images with voice-overs or text and evaluating the techniques employed by the creators.

To teach public speaking skills, teachers need to develop and introduce or review a lesson or multiple mini-lessons on such public speaking skills as articulation—enunciation and pronunciation; vocal rate, tone or volume, pitch, pacing, and inflection; making eye contact with audience members; and gestures, movement, and posture.

Designing an Assessment Rubric

In order for the choice of presentations to be equivalent, the teacher needs to design a presentation rubric that would apply to all options: I Am poetry, plot/character bags, skits or puppet shows, multimedia retellings, book trailers, or student-generated presentation formats. There should be one rubric created that can assess all presentations in the same manner, and it should assess presentation content as well as speaking skills.

It is critical that a rubric is based on focus lessons that have been taught and address the expectations defined for the presentations. Each presentation should be expected to contain the same elements but in diverse ways. Sometimes book clubs have to devise creative ways to fulfill the requirements of rubrics.

One group created and presented a movie trailer for a movie to be based on their novel. They needed to plan for a way to attain their public speaking points. In the guise of an Oprah Book Club meeting, "Oprah" introduced her book club members and the novel. The members briefly discussed the book. Then, as a special surprise for the audience, they introduced the movie trailer for the movie being made, based on the book.

Figure 6.2 is a sample rubric. Of course, teachers will adapt this rubric to their own students and lessons taught. The presentation guidelines containing the rubric are included in the appendix as figure 6A.1.

Book Club Presentation Guidelines

- Reminder: your audience has not read the novel
- Demonstrate that you have read and thought about the entire book and how it would most *effectively* be presented
- Include all major characters, setting, and plot elements: inciting incident, conflict, climax, resolution
- Everyone must have an active part in the presentation
- Presentation should be about 8-10 minutes
- Presentation must be practiced
- introduce your presentation with the title, author(s), and genre
- conclude your presentation with a short review, including author's writing craft; for which readers this would be a good match, etc.
- After the conclusion, tell the audience what your club members learned from your novel

Presentation Suggestions:
It is crucial to first summarize the story by writing out the plot (on a plot plan or a storyboard) to make sure that whichever presentation format you chose, your presentation covers all the important characters, settings, events, and decisions in the novel and that an audience who has not read the book can understand your presentation and feel like they have read the book.

Presentation Rubric—a percentage of your grade is from the group grade based on the content of your presentation and a smaller percentage is based on your individual speaking points. It is crucial that all members collaborate and share responsibilities. Below are the points to be earned.

Content (Group Points)

____/10 pts Introduction, including author, title, and genre

____/05 pts Narration to connect the scenes, objects, or presentation components

____/55 pts Literary Elements included
      ____/10 pts all major characters
      ____/05 pts crucial setting(s)
      ____/40 pts plot elements: inciting incident, conflict, climax, resolution

____/10 pts Media: appropriate choreography/choral techniques, multi-media components, objects, costumes, or other supplemental features

____/05 pts Conclusion: a brief review of the novel and what you learned from the novel

Public Speaking (Individual Points)

____/05 pts articulation: enunciation, pronunciation, and projection

____/05 pts body stance—facing audience, gestures (unless choreographed) and movement (still feet, except for choreographed movement)

____/05 pts oral skills: volume, pitch, pacing, intonation, expression

Figure 6.2.

~

CHAPTER SEVEN

Book Club Assessment

The teacher reads through a stack of journal response sheets. Yesterday she had taught a focus lesson on setting and the influence the setting might have on the plot. She asked students to note in their response journals the setting of their novels and comment on why or how it might affect the story. They were then to discuss the setting in their book club meetings. Many students made excellent points about the importance of the events of the year in which the novel took place and how that might affect the characters; some wrote about where the novel was set and how the culture of the place might come into play. All in all, the teacher felt that most students had understood and applied the point of the lesson, and she noted the names of some students with whom she will want to revisit the lesson when she next confers with readers during Reading Workshop independent reading time.

Formative Assessment

Teachers assess students and student work for many reasons. Teachers can use book clubs as formative assessment to monitor student comprehension and learning. Teachers can appreciate how to modify or adjust not only their teaching and the learning activities, if necessary, but also book club structure and procedures to help students learn better. Formative assessment may also demonstrate any need for additional differentiation for individual students.

It is a realistic fact of teaching that teachers need to accrue grades. There are a few ways that students can amass grades or, more accurately, earn points during a book club unit. Grades should reflect work accomplished, mastery of lessons taught, and the objectives or standards to be met. A summative assessment at the end of the book club should reflect the unit as a whole.

Reader Response Journals as Formative Assessment

The reader response journals introduced in chapter 5 aid teachers in understanding when the class is ready to move to more complex response by progressing from simple response starter paragraphs (see appendix figures 5A.2 and 5A.3) to double-entry journal response in which readers show the text evidence that led to their thinking (see appendix figure 5A.4). When the class has mastered simple double-entry response, the teacher can further direct response to certain aspects of the text, perhaps setting, an important event (see appendix figure 5A.6), or character traits. Readers can analyze how characters set their goals and evaluate how they handle or mishandle conflicts to achieving these goals (see appendix figure 5A.7).

Teachers are able to gather data on the effectiveness of their individual focus lessons from the class response journals. For instance, if the teacher has taught a lesson on character traits and the majority of students respond that a character is "tall" or "a good athlete" or has "long hair," the teacher will know she needs to present another whole-class lesson on character traits, differentiating them from physical traits. If only a few students' journals demonstrate that they did not comprehend the lesson topic or that they could not apply the lesson to the text being read, the teacher may elect to hold a small-group lesson with only those students during Reading Workshop independent reading time. If one student either cannot apply the lesson or was absent from class when the lesson was taught, the teacher can share these ideas when conferring with the reader during independent reading time. In this manner, the journals provide feedback to teachers on both response strategies and literary lessons to inform their teaching.

Even more important is that, based on individual response journals, teachers can monitor individual students on whether they are actually reading, how well they are comprehending what they are reading, and *if* and *how* they are interacting with and reflecting on the text. The teacher can observe exactly what is going on in the students' minds as they read and use that knowledge to generate conversations and design lessons on reading strategies.

Response journals can serve as mini-conferences with each student, and teachers can hold written conversations with those students via their journals. Students can take a few minutes to read over the teacher's comments and reflect on those comments the next day when journal entries are returned to the readers. Therefore, while teachers do not generally take part in the actual book club conversations, they can hold private conversations about the book and about their responses to their readings with individual group members.

The most fitting way to grade journals is to assign points for journal responses. Responses themselves should not be graded as reader response should be based on the reader's personal, unique, spontaneous response to the text; one reader's response is not more valid than another's, and responses are not right or wrong, although they can be either supported or not supported by the text or may be based on miscues or misreadings.

However, *whether* a reader writes a reflective response can be graded. For example, each completed journal can be assigned a certain number of points, either 100 points as a homework grade or a number of points that add up to a 100-point quiz or test grade for the entire novel reading. For example, if the book is divided into seven readings for seven book club meetings, each journal would be worth approximately fifteen points.

Another way journal points can be allotted is that each journal can contribute a number of points that total 100 points per week of book club reading. Teachers can design the systems that work best for their grading structure; the point is that there are a variety of ways to grade book club assignments and collaborations (see textbox 7.1 for an example).

Sample Book Club Unit Gradebook

November 1	Book Club Response Journal 1	15/15 pts
November 3	Book Club Response Journal 2	15/15 pts
November 5	Book Club Response Journal 3	15/15 pts
November 8	Book Club Response Journal 4	15/15 pts
November 10	Book Club Response Journal 5	15/15 pts
November 14	Book Club Response Journal 6	15/15 pts
November 16	Book Club Response Journal 7	15/15 pts
November 1	BC Meeting & Meeting Reflection 1	5/5 pts
November 3	BC Meeting & Meeting Reflection 2	5/5 pts
November 5	BC Meeting & Meeting Reflection 3	5/5 pts
November 8	BC Meeting & Meeting Reflection 4	5/5 pts
November 10	BC Meeting & Meeting Reflection 5	5/5 pts
November 14	BC Meeting & Meeting Reflection 6	5/5 pts
November 16	BC Meeting & Meeting Reflection 7	5/5 pts
Book Club Presentation x 2		200/200 pts

Textbox 7.1.

Teachers can determine exactly how they individually want journals to contribute to class grades. For example, if each journal is worth 100 points as a homework grade, for the basic double-entry journal (see appendix figure 5A.4), which has four components, each component would be worth twenty-five points for complete reflections (the right-hand column).

The more advanced double-entry journal (see appendix figures 5A.5 and 5A.6) has five sections; each would be worth twenty points. Within each journal submitted, points are accrued for the summary, the three responses, and the discussion question; in that way, only a complete journal would earn the maximum points. Teachers can allot ten points for an attempted discussion question that does not quite fit the class criteria for a good discussion question and twenty points for a discussion that meets the established criteria.

The teacher also has discretion for differentiated grading within the journal; some students may be expected to have longer, more profound responses to earn the points than other students who may not be capable of, or trained in, advanced thinking. If responses are shorter or weaker than expected from readers, those readers can be encouraged, or advised, to write and submit responses that are more appropriate for them in order to earn the maximum points in the future. Readers are not penalized for their misunderstandings, as they would be on a quiz, because they can receive full credit for completing the response journals. The teacher would point out the misunderstanding, referring to the information from the book provided in the left column.

Students who do not bring a completed journal to a book club meeting do not earn any points for the response assignment. Teachers have found that, while book club members may be annoyed by peers who are not caught up in their reading for a meeting, they are willing to allow those students to attend the meeting, especially if they had a good reason for not reading or if this happens infrequently. They know that the readers are receiving points for their journals and their nonreading peers are not (the "fairness factor").

After teachers read over and credit their responses, students add these journal sheets to their reading journals as a progressing record of the book club novel. Later, readers can refer back to these pages, and these responses become a part of their yearlong reading journals, which they can periodically analyze to assess their own reading and reading strategies for metacognitive reflection.

Meeting Reflections as Formative Assessment

Another way to assess the effectiveness of book clubs is to observe meetings. The teacher is not a participant in the book clubs but should be an active onlooker. As groups meet, teachers will want to monitor meetings and discussions by circulating and sometimes sitting in on club meetings. As they do so, they will notice whether students are following the guidelines they determined as a class for the social skills inherent in successful meetings—such as listening, taking turns, piggybacking, extending the conversation, respectful disagreeing, and including all members—and how they are demonstrating those skills (see chapter 3).

Observation will also determine if all book club members are involved in the discussions, included in the conversations, or are prepared for the meetings, and if students are on topic or on task throughout the meeting. In one class, a teacher said to her co-teacher, "Have you heard any group *not* talking about the book in the last few meetings?" Amazed, upon reflection the second teacher realized that she had not; the students were discussing the book the entire time of every meeting.

However, when observing and monitoring meetings, the teacher should assess whether the meetings are effective, what social lessons or discussion techniques may need to be reviewed, or what additional lessons and techniques might still need to be taught. The meeting reflection forms (see chapter 5) also provide feedback to both students and teachers.

Teachers may assign points for effective meetings. A sample checklist or rubric might contain topics that can be easily observed by the teacher and will be noted on student reflection forms:

- Members are participating and contributing to conversation.
- Members are being included and encouraged.
- Members are taking turns.
- Members are engaged in active listening.
- Members are using respectful language.
- Discussion comments are being extended.
- Members have their books and journals and consult both to aid discussions.

It should be made clear to students that points will not be deducted or grades for meetings will not be otherwise affected if the students self-report, on their meeting reflection forms, areas in which they need to improve.

Text Synthesis Presentations as Summative Assessment

The after-reading presentations that book clubs design, prepare, and present to their classes after reading and discussing the text are evidence of the learning and collaboration that took place through the book club format. Therefore, the presentations can be employed as summative assessments of student learning, skill acquisition, and academic achievement. Referring to the sample rubric in chapter 6, some of the skills that can be assessed are literary learning, media skills, and public speaking techniques. In this rubric, a portion of the grade is composed of a group grade and, therefore, involves the abilities inherent in effective collaboration, and a percentage of the grade is based on individual presentation skills.

Book Reviews as Individual Summative Assessment

If the teacher wishes to obtain a summative assessment that is independently completed for individual grades, following their presentations students could be required to write short critical reviews of their novels based on literary analysis lessons taught. Those reviews would be stored in a classroom binder, available for future readers who are looking for book recommendations, or submitted to a site like Goodreads or Biblionasium, providing an authentic purpose and an authentic audience for student writing.

To prepare, students would deconstruct a few sample book reviews, noting the essential elements that are included in all reviews, such as title, author, publisher, copyright date, and a very short summary, as well as discerning those elements that appear only in some reviews, for example, number of pages, awards, other books by the author, and quotations from the text. They would then each write a review of the book including the essential components in their introductory paragraphs, followed by their opinions. Reviewers would be expected to support those opinions with text evidence. Most of the necessary information could be obtained from their reading journals.

If the teacher did not wish to have five reviews of the same text, each student in the book club could write a review that contained all the essential elements and then focus their opinion on reviewing and analyzing a specific literary element—characters, setting, conflict, resolution, or theme. The reviews could then be read individually by potential readers who might be choosing a novel to read based on one particular element (e.g., setting) or collectively for those who are interested in learning about the novel as a whole.

This assignment serves to link writing with reading, the most effective way to teach the language arts. Morphing into a writing group, the book club could serve as peer reviewers and editors for each other's reviews. In the appendix as figure 7A.1 is a sample rubric.

In these various ways, a book club unit can yield grades measuring a variety of diverse skills and strategies from three sources:

- book club meetings—social and discussion skills implemented;
- individual reading journals—reading strategies and reading comprehension, as well as critical-thinking skills; and
- presentations—collaboration and academic/intellectual, technical, artistic/creative, and public speaking skills as well as providing a summative assessment of the understanding of the novel through after-reading synthesis.

Even more important than generating grades is the formative assessment that these sources provide so that teachers can adjust their teachings to expand, advance, increase, and differentiate learning for the class and for individual students.

CHAPTER EIGHT

~

Planning Book Club Reading

In one classroom, students are gathered into five book club meetings. The book clubs are reading different titles, but each is reading a verse novel. In another classroom, students are also reading in book clubs. Each book club is reading a different novel, but the members of each book club are reading a novel featuring a character or characters who are refugees from war-torn countries. One club is reading a graphic novel, one is reading a verse novel, two are reading prose novels, and one club is reading a short story anthology. In yet a third classroom, second graders are arranged in book clubs; each book club is reading a different picture book, but all the picture books were written by the same author. Some books are fiction, and some are nonfiction.

In English/language arts classes, many times out of necessity, teachers gather four to five copies of any five to six novels to which they have access for book club reading. However, even when the books are random selections, the teachers can present focus lessons on reading strategies and author craft. If the book selections are all fiction, Reading Workshop focus lessons can teach, review, or explore literacy elements and devices more deeply. If they are nonfiction, lessons can focus on main ideas and supporting details, text features, text structure, and technical vocabulary.

The primary consideration is to include books of a variety of reading levels that would appeal to different readers. Another consideration may be to choose novels that feature diverse major characters or settings and novels or informational books written by diverse authors, unless an author study is the purpose of the book club reading.

However, providing a relationship between the readings of all the book clubs promotes additional interaction among book clubs, making "big picture" thinking and learning possible. When the books for the clubs have similarities, whole-class lessons are easier to prepare, and students can also not only meet with their book clubs but also can hold inter–book club meetings in which one person from each book club meets together to compare and contrast the elements being discussed in the focus lesson, such as character traits.

If teachers are able to select the books they will utilize for book clubs, there are a variety of ways to plan book club reading. Some ways teachers can design book club reading are by genre, format, theme, topic, issues, or author.

Genre Book Clubs

One way to select books for book club reading is to choose books of the same genre for each club. "Genre" can be defined in multiple ways. The major literary genres are prose, poetry, and drama; some have added nonfiction and media. However, having five categories produces more chance of overlap, such as nonfiction written in verse. Poetry clubs will be discussed as options in chapter 9. Nonfiction or informational books for text clubs will also be discussed in chapter 9.

Since dramas are written to be performed, plays will not be considered for book clubs for these purposes; however, it would be possible to hold "drama clubs" where the students read and perform plays—first in their clubs as they read through the play and then performing the play or excerpts from the play for the class.

Book clubs, or novel clubs, can be based on literary subgenres or genres based on subject matter, such as romance, fantasy, dystopian literature, science fiction, adventure, mystery, horror, historical fiction, biographical fiction, realistic fiction, street life, folklore, and humor. Many classroom libraries and school libraries are now classified or arranged by these genres.

If the class is focusing on the reading strategies of inference and prediction, novels that are primarily mysteries could be chosen for the book clubs so that the students could practice these strategies, which are important in following, or solving, a mystery.

Fantasy novels might lend themselves to focus lessons on setting and the manner in which authors develop their fantasy worlds. Called "world building," fantasy writers each design and meticulously develop a new, original world with its own landscape, natural laws, societal customs, system of government, and magical systems governed by established rules. Minus the magic, dystopian novels afford many of the same lessons.

These categories many times overlap, but novels could be chosen by what would be considered their "primary" classification and with the focus lessons to be taught in mind. For example, since many of the major characters were vampires and werewolves, the books in the *Twilight* series would be considered fantasy, but the series also followed the romance between Bella and Edward. Therefore, *Twilight* could be matched with other romances or other fantasy novels, depending on whether the teacher was planning lessons on character traits and character motivation or leading into a reading of *Romeo and Juliet*, or if the unit was based on lessons on setting and fantasy writing or preceding or following a folklore unit.

It can also be of interest to the class members, especially the more reluctant readers, to plan book clubs that are each reading a different subgenre. That way some books will appeal to all readers, and readers from different book clubs can compare how characters, settings, and plot elements function in different genres.

Format Book Clubs: Verse Novels

Novels are written in a variety of formats. Although prose is still more common, in the last five to ten years, verse novels have become very popular in all subject genres, especially for adolescent readers. Many picture books are actually written in free verse, and some are written in rhyming verse. Verse novels, such as *Little Dog Lost*, *Love That Dog*, *Like Pickle Juice on a Cookie*, *The Wild Book*, and *Gone Fishing*, are becoming increasingly more available for young readers.

Verse novels entice "reluctant" readers because the words are less dense on the page. One adolescent who read and finished K. A. Holt's verse novel *House Arrest*, the first novel he had actually read through after years of fake reading, announced, "I just read a 300-page book! Of course, it really wasn't that long because the words didn't cover the whole page, but I just read my first 300-page book!" Also, once they get over the shock that they are reading poetry, readers fall into the rhythm and the words flow for them. English Language Learners may find verse novels easier to read for the same reasons—less dense text and shorter lines. Proficient readers find verse novels more lyrical and appreciate the artistry and the effectiveness of the line breaks.

Some novels-in-verse are written in free verse throughout the novel, but a few are written in a specific poetic format, such as Nikki Grimes's *Garvey's*

Choice, which is written in tanka. A number of verse novels are written in multiform poetry; they not only contain free verse but also portions are written in concrete or shape poetry, sonnets, haiku, tanka, cinquain, acrostic poetry, couplets, and rhyming lines, as well as less known poetic forms.

Some popular examples are Jacqueline Woodson's *Locomotion*, where the character Lonnie writes primarily in free verse but also includes a sonnet, an epistle, a list poem, and a haiku; Ron Koertig's *Shakespeare, Bats, Cleanup*, in which the narrator purposefully writes in different poetic forms he is learning from one of his father's books; and Laura Shovan's *The Last Fifth Grade of Emerson Elementary*, where each student narrator writes in different poetic form. In *Forget Me Not*, author Carolee Dean carefully orchestrates diverse poetry forms, such as villanelle, pantoum, cinquain, blank verse, and shape poems to subtly change the mood and pace of the story; and there are also scenes written in script format. Book clubs built around novels that include multiple poetic forms lend themselves to deep conversations about poetry.

Blending genres, Sharon Creech's novel *Moo* includes free verse, concrete poetry, and even prose. Likewise, in Ellie Terry's *Forget Me Not*, the narration of one character, Jinsong, is written in prose while Callie's chapters are written in free verse, a technique also used by Gae Polisner in *The Memory of Things* and in Cordelia Jensen and Laurie Morrison's *Every Shiny Thing*. These diverse formats give readers much to discuss as they analyze author's craft and infer and analyze reasons why the author may have made certain decisions, whether those decisions affected meaning, and how effective those decisions were.

There are many lessons that are intrinsic in reading verse novels. Evident are lessons about poetry and poetic devices: types of poetry, figurative language, and word choice. Poetry is, according to Samuel Taylor Coleridge, "the best words in the best order." Line breaks and the way they add more nuanced meaning is another lesson central to free verse.

Format Book Clubs: Graphic Novels

Rising rapidly in popularity are graphic novels written for all ages and reading levels. Illustrations make it easier for readers to visualize the characters, setting, and the plot events of the text. However, graphic novels require that readers read and comprehend not only the text but also read and comprehend the graphics in conjunction with the text. We live in a visual culture. Visual literacy is an important skill for our students to acquire as they are increasingly bombarded by media of all types, especially by visual messages.

Graphic novels motivate reluctant readers and engage developing readers and students who are English Language Learners because there is less written text on the page and the graphics aid comprehension of the written text. These novels employ the same reading strategies as traditional books, especially inference; readers develop critical literacy skills as they incorporate thinking about the text in conjunction with the graphics. And like traditional novels, graphic novels can have complex characters, settings, plots, and conflicts and lend themselves to the same literacy lessons as other novels. Teachers can create graphic novel book clubs, and design and sequencing, as well as studying the use of space, color, and art forms, can be built around visual reading lessons.

Many popular novels have been rewritten and published as graphic novels, including *Speak*, *Twilight*, *Stormbreaker*, and *Monster*; such classics as *To Kill a Mockingbird*, *Pride and Prejudice*, and *The Adventures of Huckleberry Finn*; and many Shakespearean plays. To take advantage of these, the teacher could construct an arrangement where one-half of the book clubs read the graphic version of a novel, paired with a club who is reading the original prose version of the same novel. In a classroom with six book clubs, the original and graphic versions of three different texts would be read. Within book clubs composed of advanced readers, half of the book club members could read the original version while the other members read the graphic version.

Classical Comics offers five graphic Shakespearean plays in three versions: original text, which presents the full Shakespeare text; plain text translated into modern English; and quick text, which has reduced dialogue for easier reading. The ten British literary fiction titles offered are available in original and quick texts. Students in different book clubs could read different versions of the same text, or students in each book club can be reading the different version of the text, allowing for heterogeneous reading proficiencies within each book club.

Multi-formatted Novels

Some novels are a blend of types of writing or of writing and illustrations or graphics, commonly referred to as multi-genre books. Some examples of these were included in the earlier section on verse novels.

Another example is Walter Dean Myers's *Monster*, which alternates chapters written as a movie script with chapters written as the journal entries of the main character. *The Dollar Kids* is written as a prose narrative but includes comic strips that help tell the story. *Nothing but the Truth* interweaves multiple genres, including memos, letters, interview transcripts, dialogue, and journal entries. And Kate Messner's newest novel, *Breakout*, is formatted as letters, Post-it Notes, announcements, lists, text messages, news articles and news reports, surveys, parodies, statistical charts, recorded conversations and interviews, notes, and graphics. Messner also includes poetry inspired by poets: name poems, haikus, golden shovel poems, and raps based on *Hamilton* lyrics.

Memoir Book Clubs

Technically, memoir is not a genre of fiction; memoir writing is narrative nonfiction since it is based on a person's life, written by that person. Thus, it is considered nonfiction but includes narrative elements. Memoir differs from autobiography, which is the chronology of the writer's entire life, a history of the author's life from its beginning to the time of the writing. Memoir primarily focuses on one aspect of the writer's life and is based on the author's remembrances, feelings, and emotions.

Memoir also involves reflection, an exploration of the experiences and memories covered by the memoir. In the classroom, memoir can provide a bridge between fiction and nonfiction texts for readers, combining elements of both types of writing and requiring strategies employed in both types of reading (Roessing, 2014).

Memoir is particularly effective for book clubs because memoirs are available in a continuum of reading levels, in a variety of formats, and on a variety of subjects; they also feature diverse authors and settings. Memoirs are appropriate for beginning readers to advanced readers.

There are many picture-book memoirs, such as *Coat of Many Colors*, *When I Was Young in the Mountains*, *Bigmama's*, *Saturdays and Teacakes*, and *Passage to Freedom: The Sugihara Story*. There are also a variety of chapter-book memoirs for developing readers, such as *26 Fairmount Avenue* and *Marshfield Dreams*, in addition to memoirs for middle-grade and young adult readers. More than 150 memoirs for grades 5–12 as well as picture books and memoir poetry that can be utilized as mentor texts are listed in *Bridging the Gap: Reading Critically and Writing Meaningfully to Get to the Core* (Roessing, 2014), and there have been a proliferation of memoirs published since then.

Patricia Polacco has written numerous picture books that are memoirs of her childhood, such as *Thank You, Mr. Falkner*; *Meteor*; *My Rotten Redheaded Older Brother*; *My Ol' Man*; *Thunder Cake*; *The Junkyard Wonders*; *An "A" from Miss Keller*; and *Some Birthday!*. An advantage is that Polacco illustrates her own books, and the illustrations become a part of the author's text. Her picture books are written at a variety of reading levels, and there are sufficient titles for each book club to read a different memoir.

There also are memoir collections for students who would be more engaged with shorter writings or to introduce a unit on memoir reading. *When I Was Your Age: Original Stories about Growing Up*, volumes 1 and 2, include short memoir essays by authors familiar to young adolescent readers, such as Katherine Paterson, Walter Dean Myers, Joseph Bruchac, Jane Yolen, and James Howe. Other memoir anthologies featuring short memoirs by diverse authors familiar to adolescent readers are *Sixteen: Stories about That Sweet and Bitter Birthday* and *Dear Bully: Seventy Authors Tell Their Stories*.

Many memoirs have been written in free verse, such as Margarita Engle's *Enchanted Air*, appropriate for young readers, and its companion book for more mature readers, *Soaring Earth*; this format can be enticing to reluctant readers. Sonya Sones's memoir of her thirteenth year, *Stop Pretending: What Happened When My Big Sister Went Crazy*, and Jacqueline Woodson's *Brown Girl Dreaming*, appropriate for middle-grade readers, are also very powerful in their verse imagery and word choice.

Increasingly, memoirs are also available in graphic format. There are now quite a few appropriate for adolescent readers, including *Tomboy, Honor Girl, Persepolis: The Story of a Childhood, Amazing Fantastic Incredible: A Marvelous Memoir* (about Stan Lee's career at Marvel for comic book fans), and the newly published National Book Award finalist *Hey, Kiddo*. For younger readers, there are fewer graphic memoirs available, but some that have become popular include *El Deafo, Real Friends, Smile*, and, by the same author, *Sisters*.

Memoirs have been written on such divergent topics as sports, mental illness, family relationships, fame, abuse, and championships. Authors of memoirs include models, athletes, dancers, soldiers, refugees, actors, Nobel Prize winners, singers, and teens—literally anyone a reader could identify with or be curious about. This is one compelling reason they engage readers. Memoir generates profound conversations within and among book clubs.

Another advantage is that memoir reading in book clubs can be paired with memoir writing. While book club members are reading memoirs and studying the author's craft, students write their own memoirs, using the memoirs read as mentor texts (Roessing, 2014).

Thematic Book Clubs

One of the most common approaches to plan book club book selections is to organize around common themes. Each club reads a different novel, which could be written in a different genre or format, that relates to the theme.

Common themes are survival, coming of age, relationships, social justice, moral dilemmas, heroism, quests, and love.

Another thematic basis for book clubs would be issues that children and adolescents are navigating in their lives: family relationships; peer relationships; adversity and bullying; prejudice and racism; facing challenges; handling mental illness; physical disabilities and neurodiversity; surviving loss and trauma; resilience; sexuality and gender identification; and identity and self-discovery. When reading books that contain these issues, readers have conversations beyond the books, and the books are employed as mirrors in which readers may see themselves represented and therefore valued; as maps by which readers learn ways to successfully, and unsuccessfully, navigate life; or as windows through which readers can gain understanding of and empathy for those they may view as different from themselves.

Teachers can present lessons and research on some of these issues—for example, under the theme of "facing challenges," information on homelessness, incarcerated parents, poverty, and foster placements—or task book clubs with conducting research to complement their after-reading presentations to the class. When students conduct inter–book club meetings, they can compare their characters and plots as they relate to or are affected by the issue.

Topic Book Clubs

Topic book clubs are not remarkably different from thematic book clubs but are based on more specific topics, for example, the Holocaust, genocide, refugees, environment, or Asia. Commonly, these topics will relate to disciplinary studies and, therefore, will be discussed further in chapter 9 and provide the sample unit in chapter 10.

Author-Study Book Clubs

Another way to employ book clubs is for an author study. The most effective way to design this type of unit is for the whole class to read and analyze one book by the author; that book will then serve as the mentor text for the author study, a point of comparison for the other novels being read. The mentor text can be used as a read-aloud by the teacher who then facilitates whole-class discussions, or, more effectively, the novel is read by the entire class individually and discussed in whole-class discussions or discussed in small groups in preparation for the book club reading that will follow. The teacher can use this text to teach the social skills lessons and to model and teach the reader response strategies that the students will use in their upcoming book clubs.

Following the whole-class novel, students will choose their book club texts from a selection of books written by the same author in the manner described in chapter 2. It is advantageous to choose an author who writes in a variety of genres so that each book club can read a different genre while comparing and contrasting the author's style to the mentor text and to the novels being read by the other book clubs.

For middle grades and high school, one author in particular comes to mind. Walter Dean Myers wrote more than 100 books for beginning to advanced readers at a variety of reading levels in diverse subject genres: memoir, street life or moral dilemmas, romance, historical fiction, sports fiction, and biographies. He also wrote novels in a variety of formats, such as picture books and short story collections, and one of his novels, *Monster*, has been rewritten as a graphic novel.

Another author who has written quite a few early reader, middle-grade, and young adult novels in various reading levels and somewhat different genres is Jacqueline Woodson. There are many other authors who would work well as the subjects of author studies.

Author study can be organized with each book club reading a short story collection written by one author, such as Walter Dean Myers's *145th Street*, Beverley Naidoo's *Out of Bounds: Seven Stories of Conflict and Hope*, and *Skin and Other Stories* by Roald Dahl.

For younger readers, Patricia Polacco has written approximately fifty picture books—memoirs (as mentioned earlier in this chapter), historical fiction, family-history stories, cultural stories, an ABC book, stories about diversity, folktales, and humorous stories—at diverse reading levels. In addition, since Polacco illustrates her own books, the artistic techniques and styles also can be compared and contrasted.

When conducting an author study, in addition to analyzing and comparing the characters the author creates, the plots the author fabricates, and the settings, readers will want to examine the author's craft, or how the author writes. Readers will explore the distinct techniques the author uses across novels, even novels of different genres and formats. Readers can complete a double-entry author's craft form included in the appendix as figure 8A.1, Book Club Double-Entry Author's Craft Journal, for one response per week during the reading of the novel while using other double-entry forms described in chapter 5 and included in the appendix for their other readings of the novel during the week.

Book club reading can achieve many academic and affective goals, but a crucial function is to generate important conversations in a supportive reading atmosphere. Structuring the reading so that readers each read a text that is interesting to and appropriate for them and stretches their thinking—a text that leads to discussions not only within their book clubs but also connecting with readers in other book clubs (whether by genre, format, theme, topic, or author)—makes the experience much more valuable.

CHAPTER NINE

Text Clubs across the Curriculum

They sit in circles, looking through their notes and paging through books, talking and sharing questions. As one student talks, others nod; some point to passages in their texts. This could be a book club meeting in any elementary or secondary English/language arts classroom, but it is not. It is a university classroom, and their books are textbooks. In a secondary social studies class, students are arranged in small clusters, and each group is reading informational books about a different war; in science, each text club is reading multiple articles on a different topic from the unit; and the health class students in each text club are reading novels. An English/ language arts class is divided into small-group poetry clubs, and each student is reading poetry by one of the poets of the Harlem Renaissance.

The book club concept and format can expand across the curriculum and incorporate different types of text, not only literary fiction but also informational texts, articles, poetry, and even school textbooks. Book clubs can become "text clubs," where students meet in small collaborative groups who read the same text and discuss that text, presenting it in some way to the rest of the class. Text clubs, even with short texts, offer the same benefits as book clubs featuring novels.

Literary Book Clubs

Of course, that being said, there is always a place of value for novels in many disciplines. Although many disciplinary teachers may feel that there is not enough time to cover state standards *and* read novels in their classes, they may be surprised how much content students learn and how many standards they meet through novel book club reading and the ensuing discussions. And when students in each club read and present on a different novel, feasibly on a different topic covered in the curriculum, the class as a whole learns from the reading of all the novels. Presentations can be modified from those described in chapter 6 to focus more on the topic than on the characters and plot.

Book clubs in content area classes, such as social studies/history, science, or health can meet every other day or once or twice a week. Even though content area teachers may not follow Reading Workshop guidelines as presented in chapter 4, a focus lesson, based on the disciplinary content, can be taught at the beginning of each book club meeting class, and members can be required to connect the lesson to their novels and their book club discussions.

Social Studies/History Classes

One of the most effective ways to learn about any historical event, and the nuances and effects of those events, is through a novel study—the power of story. When asked, students in social studies classes object to the fact that they only read textbooks; they explain that they desire information that helps them make sense of what they are reading and learning. When reading historical novels, they say that they truly understand the impact of such events on ordinary people living in extraordinary times and the places in which they live. For social studies or history classes, there are countless novels written on a variety of topics. And novels show the perspectives of those affected by the historic events. Reading novels in book clubs allows the class to hear about books written from divergent perspectives, such as the novels chosen for the 9/11 unit shared in chapter 10.

Students in each book club could read a different novel on one topic being studied in the curriculum. For instance, if the curriculum introduced apartheid in South Africa, book clubs could choose from *Waiting for the Rain*; *The Power of One*; *Chain of Fire*; *Cry, the Beloved Country*; *When Morning Comes*; and *Kaffir Boy: An Autobiography*. Each of these books covers a different time period under apartheid, and they are written at diverse reading levels.

As an alternative, each book club could read a novel that focused on a different topic that was studied in the curriculum during the year. One book club could read a novel that is set during World War I, one during the Spanish Civil War or during the Great Depression, one during World War II, one during the Holocaust, and one during Apartheid.

As another option, the teacher could choose a wide-ranging issue that the class will discuss over the course. For example, under contemporary wars and genocide, middle-grade book clubs could read novels such as *A Long Walk to Water*, about the Sudanese genocide; *Tree Girl*, about the genocide in Guatemala; *The Day of the Pelican*, about the Serbian oppression of Kosovo; *Long Way Gone: Memoirs of a Boy Soldier*, the memoir of a child soldier in the civil war in Sierra Leone; and *Child Soldier: When Boys and Girls Are Used in War*, a graphic memoir of a boy soldier in the Democratic Republic of the Congo in 1993. A book club novel unit based on the study of 9/11 is presented in chapter 10 as a sample unit employing book clubs.

Book clubs are also ideal for reading novels that take place in various locales for studies of geography or world cultures. Book clubs with younger readers can read different variants of the Cinderella story, which has been traced across the globe and to different ethnic and socioeconomic groups within continents and countries (Roessing, 2012). By presenting authentic information about the geography, environment, government, family structure, food, clothing, class system, rituals, and values of a culture, folktales help children better understand cultures of diverse times and places, acknowledge their interrelatedness, and develop an appreciation for the customs and beliefs of different peoples.

In social studies classes, the students might focus on one geographical area or continent, each group collaboratively reading a Cinderella variant from a different ethnic culture within that continent while researching the culture to appreciate examples of the culture reflected in the folktale. If the curriculum covers Asia, there are original Cinderella variants from many Asian countries and cultures, for example, Vietnam, India, Korea, Thailand, Japan, China, Cambodia, and the Hmong people. In a curriculum covering world cultures, each book club might read a variant from a different geographical area, for example, Europe, Asia, the Soviet countries, Africa, the Middle East, and the United States.

Clubs can compare stories and cultures in inter–book club meetings or through after-reading presentations. In one fifth-grade class reading Cinderella variants, a young man whose book club had read, researched, discussed, and presented a Japanese variant intently watched a video version of *Yeh-Shen*, a Cinderella story from China. Afterward, the teacher overheard him musing, "Being both Asian countries, I would have expected *Yeh-Shen* to be more like our Japanese tale. I will have to research the Chinese culture to find out why it was so different."

Science Classes

In science classes, there may not be as apparent a correlation between curriculum and novels. But there are novels about such unlikely subjects as infectious disease, such as *Code Orange* (smallpox); *Fever, 1793* (yellow fever); *Chasing Secrets* (bubonic plague); *The Great Trouble: A Mystery of London, the Blue Death, and a Boy Called Eel* (cholera); *A Death-Struck Year* (Spanish influenza); *This Thing Called the Future* (AIDS); and *Extraordinary Means* (drug-resistant tuberculosis) written for middle school/high school readers. For upper elementary grades, Carl Hiaasen's novels, *Hoot, Scat, Flush,* and *Chomp* focus on environmental issues.

Moreover, reading science fiction is an inviting way to hook prospective scientists into thinking *What if . . .* Science fiction has a relationship with the principles of science; science fiction stories involve partially fictitious, but partially true, laws or theories of science and their impact on individuals or society. As Merriam-Webster defines it, science fiction has a scientific factor as an essential orienting component. In other words, science fiction needs to make sense within the natural laws of the universe and, therefore, complements the study of those natural laws and science.

Health Classes

A university class of pre-service health and physical education teachers, studying the benefits of implementing book clubs and using young adult literature in their future health classes, read novels that included a variety of health issues in book clubs (Long and Roessing, 2015). Students chose topics that included steroid use among teen athletes, sports-related concussion and chronic traumatic encephalopathy (CTE), eating disorders and body image, and teen pregnancy.

As a departure from traditional book clubs, some of the students in one class opted to read a variety of novels in their book clubs. Within the four-member book club reading about steroid use, the two male students elected to read *Gym Candy*, a novel that features a male adolescent protagonist, while the two female group members decided to read *Boost*, the story centering on a female basketball player.

Another group, reading novels about eating disorders and body image, chose two books, *Perfect: A Novel* and a memoir, *Stick Figure: A Diary of My Former Self*, for their group of five. The three-member book club examining teen pregnancy decided to each read a different novel, choosing *After*, *The First Part Last*, and *Annie's Baby: The Diary of Anonymous, a Pregnant Teenager*, while all four members of the fourth book club read *Pop*, Gordon Korman's novel about CTE from sports-related concussions.

As college juniors and seniors, these students were proficient readers and experienced at self-directed learning and discussion techniques and, therefore, able to read different novels within the same group while tailoring their conversations to issues that all the novels presented and analyzing ways in which different characters handled, or mishandled, their issues. They also focused on how their health issues were presented in different novels. Younger students may do better with the traditional approach of one novel per book club.

For their group presentations, these college students were required to research the health issue addressed in their chosen books and include the research in class presentations, consequently learning even more about the issue themselves and from their peers. Presentations were made not only in some of the formats described in chapter 6 but also as documentaries and talk shows.

Students in the two health education classes wrote in a post-project survey that "Reading YA literature on the health issue provided a better understanding of the selected health issue . . . [and] brought greater realism to the issue—a personal perspective and story that extended beyond facts, data, and statistics" (Long and Roessing, 2015).

Informational Text Clubs

Very appropriate for content area courses would be using informational texts that cover topics in the curriculum. There are many advantages of reading an informational text to supplement textbook reading:

- A book, even a short book or an advanced picture book, offers more information on the topic than is included in a textbook chapter and increases learning of topics and concepts.
- Informational books can complement textbooks and enrich and extend learning.
- Trade books are written with the audience, rather than the textbook purchasers, in mind.
- Informational texts are written by authors who craft their writings and can be employed as mentor texts for informative writings.
- There are informational texts available at all reading levels for differentiation, compared to a textbook that is written at one reading level that is frequently above the level of the majority of class readers since they have little or no background knowledge on the topic.
- Books often provide multiple perspectives on topics.

- Many textbooks are out of date, especially in science; it is easy to find current informational trade books on any topic.
- Well-written informational books engage the reader and, in so doing, may expand interest in the topic.
- Increasingly, many schools are moving away from employing textbooks in their curricula; informational books provide support of the topic study as well as experience in disciplinary reading.
- Informational trade books are available in multiple genres—prose, poetry, graphic, and reader's theater scripts, for example—and support individual tastes in reading.

Informational book clubs (or "text clubs," the term "book clubs" has been used to specify literary texts in chapters 1–8) would operate in the same way as book clubs reading novels. The teachers would offer a variety of books on the disciplinary unit topic in different genres and/or different reading levels: World War II (social studies), weather (science), Shakespeare (English/language arts), mental health (health), and even geometry (math). Or books on different topics within a unit would be offered, such as for the science unit "Changing Landforms," books are available about hurricanes, volcanoes and eruptions, earthquakes, floods and tsunamis, landslides and avalanches, and wildfires.

Students would peruse the texts as outlined in chapter 2 and choose a text that would place them in a particular text club that is reading that text. Students then meet in text clubs to plan the reading schedule for their books. Text clubs would meet for about fifteen minutes every other day or twice a week to discuss and jot down what they learned. With a few modifications, the same basic double-entry journal first introduced for book club novel response can be adapted and employed for informational text; a reproducible form is included in the appendix as figure 9A.1, Informational Text Club Double-Entry Journal.

After reading their texts, each text club would plan a short presentation to the class, especially in those classes where text clubs each read about distinct topics within a unit. Rather than oral presentations, clubs might collaborate on creating their own informational text, composing a newspaper, a pamphlet, or an ABC book on their topic to share with class members.

As an alternative whole-class project, the text clubs could cooperatively produce a magazine based on the unit focus, such as the *Renaissance Report: Special Shakespearean Issue*. Each text club would contribute a section on their topic—Elizabethan England, Elizabethan fashions, Shakespeare's life, Shakespeare's plays, the Globe Theatre, Shakespeare's language—and the magazine would be composed of a variety of articles in diverse writing styles. Each club could create magazine advertisements based on their topics, additionally including other typical magazine pages, such as reviews and interviews.

The type of presentation may depend on the timing of the text clubs. Text clubs readings and meetings could be held in preparation for an upcoming unit of study, held concurrently with the unit of study, or held after, as an extension to the unit of study. If held before the unit was taught, a written presentation handout that would provide background information and support student learning would be beneficial. If presented after the unit, the presenters would be expected to make connections to the unit. After-reading presentations could be written or performed.

Article Clubs

Sometimes teachers only want students to read articles, rather than a book, on a curricular topic. There are news, magazine, and journal articles, as well as articles from websites that are written on a variety of reading levels and lengths, as well as in diverse formats.

The teacher can group students into article clubs; these clubs would continue for the length of the unit and possibly shift for the next unit. The teacher may group students homogeneously, assigning more challenging articles to the more proficient readers. Alternatively, the groups can be composed heterogeneously based on student interests, especially when teachers can obtain articles that are written on multiple levels, such as articles published on Newsela, a database of current events stories that can be accessed by reading level.

The teacher can assign articles to groups; interest in the topic is of less significance than in book club reading since students will be only reading short texts, rather than working through an entire novel or an informational book. However, groups can be created based on topic interest, or groups, when formed, can be given the opportunity to choose their article topics.

For example, when studying the Holocaust and reading articles supplementary to the textbook, at the beginning of the unit article clubs could read articles on such topics as the Nazi Party, Nazi propaganda, or the Nuremberg Laws. During the unit, students could study articles about the different concentration camps, the Righteous Gentiles, and resistance groups. At the end of the unit, clubs could read supplementary information on liberation, the Nuremberg trials, Holocaust victims, Holocaust heroes, and displaced persons. In classes, such as science, where the curriculum may not include a textbook, articles would be particularly useful.

Article clubs would generally meet one or two times to read and discuss articles, depending on whether the groups each had one long article or had multiple articles on a topic and how much of the class time the teacher wished to reserve for article clubs. Students would read and annotate the article(s) and then meet in their article clubs and hold discussions. To present ideas learned to the rest of the class, the class would then plan a jigsaw activity, an efficient and cooperative way to learn material.

For a jigsaw activity, each article club receives a number: 1, 2, 3, 4, and 5. Following the social skills taught for book clubs or introducing these skills as outlined in chapter 3, the members of each club would come to a consensus on the most important points or facts from their article(s) that they will share with their classmates in the other article clubs. Students would next move into inter-club groups formed of one member from each article club. In other words, each inter-club group would have five members—one from each article club (1, 2, 3, 4, and 5)—and each member would present the agreed-upon information from their article(s), alleviating the need for all class members to read all articles.

Since the article club members had decided exactly what they would present, all groups will receive the same information. Groups then can have a short time to hold a discussion, which will be different in each inter-club group. If a person is absent when students meet in inter-club groups, or if there is one less member in an article club group, one of the students with that number can fill in at the end of the meeting, or the teacher can substitute. Each article club is a piece of the puzzle, and, in their inter-club group, students put the pieces together to construct the whole puzzle "picture."

Poetry Clubs

Poetry clubs would be organized much like article clubs. Clubs can be formed for the duration of a poetry unit or could gather whenever poetry is being employed in English/language arts or in the content area classes. Members would read poems individually, annotating while reading, and then hold club conversations. For a presentation, poetry clubs could simply present a favorite poem, possibly adding some choreography or movement, and employ some of the choral techniques explained in chapter 6. They might also provide a PowerPoint slide backdrop of images to accompany their interpretations and share the most significant points of their discussions.

Textbook Clubs

The majority of the time, textbooks are read independently, frequently as homework. It is well documented that most textbooks are not particularly reader friendly; they are filled with an overload of new concepts and disciplinary language and, in many cases, writing that is not well crafted or engaging to readers. And textbooks are not differentiated in any way. Frequently, students do not understand what they read, or they come to class with unanswered questions.

Many students, especially readers who are less than proficient, do not know how to extract key information from text; they assume everything is important because "it is in a textbook." Also some students are not able to comprehend the way information may be presented, such as in tables and charts, in a textbook. However, for academic success, especially in college, and for future reading of technical manuals and informational materials, students need to become effective and strategic textbook readers.

Textbook clubs provide a time and place for students to gather with their peers and discuss the textbook chapters assigned and to collaboratively find answers to questions and to correct misconceptions. Textbook clubs are one approach where it may be advantageous to group students heterogeneously. These clubs are more akin to literature circles because all students are reading the same text, and therefore, students can be moved around during the term or year.

Textbook clubs meet the first ten minutes of class to review their notes or annotations and discuss misconceptions and unanswered questions. Students can collaborate to discern the answers to any questions they may all have and to determine key concepts and meaning. Discussing the chapter prepares students for the ensuing class and supports student learning.

If any questions remain after the discussion, the textbook clubs can list them on the board, and if another textbook club has had the same conversation and arrived at an answer, or if another club member can explain, they may do so as class begins. From the list, the teacher will know where to begin or what to include in the day's lesson. In this same way, textbook clubs have been employed successfully in college and graduate-level courses.

Text clubs, such as those described in this chapter, have all the advantages of book clubs: increased comprehension, motivation, and engagement; collaboration and employment of social skills; and, in many situations, choice and differentiated text. Text clubs feature student-led discussions, leading to increased speaking and listening skills, and are adaptable to texts of any format and length; text clubs can benefit readers in classes across the curriculum.

CHAPTER TEN

~

A Sample Book Club Unit

The 9/11 Novel Unit

Every historical event is distinct and affects people and places uniquely—and each event is surrounded by misconceptions, misunderstandings, miscommunications, and differing and shifting perspectives. But no historical event may be as unique and complicated as the study of the events of September 11, 2001. One reason is that none of our current K–12 students were alive at the time of this event. Although true for most historic events, in the case of 9/11 the teachers tasked with presenting this topic bore witness to this day and the days that followed. In that way, the events of 9/11 are exceptional to teach and talk about.

Also many of these students' parents and relatives are currently serving in the Middle East as part of the U.S. response to these terrorist attacks; however, many children do not recognize the connections between the events of September 11, 2001, and the present actions of our military in the Middle East. When the subject is introduced, teachers have noted that some students have said, "Why are we still talking about 9/11? It's over." With the devastation and impact of these events on past, present, and future relations and as ingrained a part of history these events are, they need to be discussed and understood as much as possible.

Studying 9/11 through stories—novels read and discussed in book clubs in English/language arts or social studies/history classes—is most effective. When those of us who were present during this time talk about 9/11, we share our personal stories of the day and the days that followed; we talk about how these events affected us, our friends, our relatives, strangers, our towns, and the nation and world as a whole. When classes read novels about 9/11, especially in book clubs where small groups of students are reading different novels, they not only access many differing perspectives to a story within their own book club but also can compare stories with other book clubs.

What follows is a sample 9/11 unit based on novels read through book clubs adapted by the author and facilitated with diverse classes in grades 5 through 9 in six schools in both English/language arts and social studies/history classes. These plans are based on seventy-five-minute to ninety-minute class periods but can easily be adapted for shorter class times. In English/language arts, the book clubs met every other day for four weeks; in social studies/history classes, they met twice a week for four weeks.

9/11 Units in English/Language Arts Classes

Day 1

1. The teacher hands out KWHLR charts. This chart is an adaptation of the traditional KWL chart and can be used throughout the unit (see figures 10.1 and 10.2). There are five columns on the chart for students to write down
   - What I *Know*
   - What I *Want* to Know
   - *How*/Where I Can Find Out
   - What I *Learned*
   - My *Reflections* on What I Learned

Study of the Events and Effects of SEPTEMBER 11, 2001		
What I KNOW What I Think I May KNOW or Heard	What I WANT to Know/Learn My Questions	HOW/Where I Can Find Out Who I Can Interview

Figure 10.1.

Study of the Events and Effects of SEPTEMBER 11, 2001	
What I LEARNED	My THOUGHTS About What I Learned New Questions From What I Learned

Figure 10.2.

2. The teacher instructs students, "On your chart, in the first column, write down what you know, what you think you know, or what you have heard about 9/11. You can write down names, places, dates, and events. You may write a lot of facts or you may only know a few facts to write down. Do not worry about being 'wrong.' Some things you write down may be accurate, and some may turn out be inaccurate."

3. After students are finished filling in their first column, the teacher continues:
   - "After you have finished writing down what you know or think you may know, write down any questions you have or what you want to know in the second column. The less you have in the first column, the more questions you will probably have in the second column."
   - "Now, in the third column, write down where you might be able find the answers to your questions; make a list of sources and people."

4. The students watch the *Nick News* video, "What Happened: The Story of September 11, 2011," about the 9/11 attacks, narrated by Linda Ellerbee. They are directed to add what they learned and any new questions to their charts.

5. The teacher book talks the novels that are choices for their book clubs. Depending on the grade level and class size, four or five of the following novels are offered. Each of these novels offers a different perspective of the events and effects of the 9/11 attacks. The majority of the novels include characters who are diverse in some respect—ethnicity, race, religion, generation, or geography.
   - *Eleven* by Tom Rogers (grades 5–8) is about a boy who is turning eleven on 9/11/2001. When the planes hit the Towers, Alex is left to take care of his little sister and a stray dog he has adopted, wondering if his father will return, and comforting Mac, a lonely man who is awaiting his only son's return from the Towers. This novel is a powerful examination of the events of 9/11 and how they affected ordinary people—and one boy's birthday.
   - *Towers Falling* by Jewell Parker Rhodes (grades 5–8) takes place in 2016 where a young teacher is grappling with teaching the events of 9/11 to students who were not even born at the time. The fifth-grade characters explore "What does it mean to be an American?" as well as why history is relevant, alive, and, especially, personal, as three students—one black, one white, one Muslim—explore the effects of the events of 9/11 on each of their families. Déja's "journey of discovery" about the falling of the Towers helps her father work through his connection to the event and his resulting post-traumatic stress disorder (PTSD).

- *Nine, Ten: A September 11 Story* by Nora Raleigh Baskin (grades 5–8) is set during the days leading up to 9/11—in Brooklyn, Los Angeles, Columbus, and Shanksville where readers follow four diverse middle-grade students, black, white, Jewish, and Muslim, who are affected by the events of 9/11. Sergio, Will, Aimee, and Naheed first cross paths in the O'Hare Airport on September 9, 2001, and converge yet again at Ground Zero on September 11, 2002; each are there for different reasons, but this time their paths leading them back together have meaning.
- *Just a Drop of Water* by Kerry O'Malley Cerra (grades 5–9) follows friends Jake Green and Sameed Madina who live in a Florida town where one of the terrorists has been arrested. Sam's father, a Muslim whose business card the terrorist was carrying, comes under FBI surveillance, and the neighborhood divides in their support. The school bullies begin to refer to Sam as a "towelhead" and attack the local mosque. This novel examines the Islamophobia that followed the events of 9/11.
- *Somewhere Among* by Annie Donwerth-Chikamatsu (grades 5–8), written in free verse, relates the story of fifth-grader Ema who is binational, bicultural, bilingual, and biracial. When Ema, with her mother, goes to live with her traditional Japanese grandparents from June 21, 2001, to January 2, 2002, she traverses the intricacies of fusing two distinct cultures. For example, on September 11, 2001, Ema experiences both two typhoons in her town and the terrorist attacks in America—on television.
- *All We Have Left* by Wendy Mills (grades 7–12) intertwines two stories, that of eighteen-year-old Travis and sixteen-year-old Alia, a Muslim, who were in the Towers as they fell, and the story of Travis's sister, Jesse, fifteen years later, a member of a dysfunctional family whose lives are still overwhelmingly affected by That Day. Jesse commits a racist act and learns about herself and others as she becomes friends with a Muslim boy and unravels the mystery around her brother's death.
- *The Memory of Things* by Gae Polisner (grades 8–12), told in alternating narratives—one character's in prose, the other in free verse, is the story of teenager Kyle Donahue who, after witnessing the fall of the first Twin Tower and evacuating his school, discovers a girl who is covered in ash on the Brooklyn Bridge; she has no memory of who she is. He helps her rediscover who she is, why and what she was doing on the bridge, and her connection to the events of 9/11.

- *Refugees* by Catherine Stine (grades 9–12) relates the stories of two teens on different sides of the world who are affected by the events of 9/11. Dawn is a foster teen who runs away to New York City; as she plays her flute on the streets near Ground Zero to earn money for food, she is approached by families of victims who ask her to play for the memories of their loved ones, and this becomes her mission. Johar, an Afghani teenager whose family was killed by the Taliban, flees to a refugee camp in Pakistan where he works for a Red Cross doctor, Dawn's foster mother. Dawn and Johar connect through phone calls, when Dawn calls her mother, and eventually e-mails, and the reader learns how war, the U.S. involvement, and the events of 9/11 affected those in many countries.
- *The Usual Rules* by Joyce Maynard (grades 8–12) is a novel about the effects of the events of September 11 on the families and friends of the victims—those left behind. When her mother goes to work at her job at the World Trade Center on September 11, 2001, and does not return, thirteen-year-old Wendy's world changes. The novel portrays not only the loss of Wendy, her stepfather Josh and her half brother Louie but also the suffering and uncertainty of all those left behind. As families hang signs, readers learn how different this loss was for many people who held out hope for a long time without a sense of closure.

6. A different novel is placed in front of each student in groups of four or five. Instructions are given to students to peruse and choose their book club choice novels: "Examine the book in front of you. Look at the front cover, read the back cover or the flaps and at least one page. When I say, 'Pass,' pass to the next student who has a different book. There should only be four (five) passes. When you have perused all the choices, on a piece of paper, write your name and your #1, #2, and #3 choices and a reason for your first choice."

Before the next class, the teacher assigns book clubs, based on student choice, modified by what the teacher thinks may be the most appropriate novel for students within their three choices (see chapter 2 for more information on considerations for creating book club groups).

Day 2

1. The teacher defines and describes book clubs, the agenda for book club meetings, techniques for holding discussions, and strategies for writing reflective reader response journals. If this will be the students' first book club experience, the lessons for the day include social skills and

discussion techniques as explained in chapter 3. (If the students have discussed and practiced social skills and have held successful discussions, teachers can review those skills and expectations and move on to introducing or practicing reader response journaling.)

2. (a) The focus lesson for the day is reader response. For students who are unfamiliar with reader response journals, the teacher explains reader response: "As you read your novel, you are going to keep a reader response journal. Reader response is writing down what *you* are *thinking* as you read. There is no right or wrong. You need to stop every one-third of your scheduled reading and write down three to four sentences about
   - what you are thinking,
   - questions you have,
   - connections you can make,
   - inferences or predictions, and
   - what from the text made you think this way and supports your thinking.

   "If you start each response with a 'response starter,' it will help you write your thoughts rather than a summary of the text. Sample response starters are listed on the bottom of the front page of the journal page. On the front page of your response journal page, you will write a summary of what happens, only recording important events."

   The teacher introduces the two-sided response journal included as figures 5A.2 and 5A.3 in the appendix and demonstrates response journaling through a "gradual release of responsibility" lesson by taking students through a teacher model, guided practice, and independent application based on an article about the events of 9/11, "I Was 11 on 9/11" (Modigliani, 2011).
   - Teacher Model: The teacher projects and reads the first section of the article, underlining phrases that capture her attention on the screen. She then drafts a short reflection on each underlined phrase (see textbox 10.1).
   - Guided Practice Directions: "Read sections 2 and 3 of the article. With a partner decide one fact to highlight in section 2, 'Running from Danger,' and in section 3, 'A Day of Loss.' Individually, write a three-to-four-sentence journal entry about something you highlighted, beginning with an appropriate response starter from the first page of the form."
   - Independent Application Directions: "Individually read the section titled 'After the Attacks.' Highlight a fact of interest. Write a three-

Reader Response—What I'm Thinking:

When I read the title, **I inferred** *that this was The 9/11, the day the World Trade Centers were attacked—9/11/2001. And then I saw the date at the beginning of the article and saw I had guessed correctly. The subtitle said New York City, and* **I wondered** *if Emily was in one of the schools near the Trade Center and if she saw what happened as it happened.*

I found it interesting *that the students evacuated. I would think it could have been safer inside the building than on the streets.* **This reminded** *me of the novel Up from the Sea where during the tsunami in Japan the children ran from their school, and I thought the same thing.*

I was surprised that *Emily can remember what she saw and how it felt so exactly even ten years later, but maybe that is what happens when a disaster strikes. I remember when I was rear-ended by another car more than thirty years ago. I think it is because my baby daughter was supposed to be in the back seat but I decided to leave her at home.*

Textbox 10.1.

       to-four-sentence response to that fact beginning with one response starter."

- Once the students finish reading the article the teacher can ask students, in pairs, to practice completing the summary on the first page of the response journal.

3. (b) In classes where students are familiar with reader response and have previously written reader response journals, the teacher introduces double-entry journals (figures 5A.4 and 5A.5 in the appendix). The same directions are given; however, the text evidence is written in the left column and the response is written in the right column (see figure 10.3).

4. In pairs. students design a "good" discussion question based on the article following the guidelines discussed in class (as described in chapter 3). They can then be assigned to their book clubs, meeting in their book clubs to discuss their questions.

5. The teacher announces the meeting schedule for the book clubs, emphasizing the date the reading of the novel should be completed,

Name _____ My Notes for Our Next Text Club Meeting	Text Title "I Was 11 on 9/11" Pages _____ to _____
Something I noticed in the novel (page #) (a character, something about the setting, an event, a decision, a quote from the text)	What I am thinking about that... (questions, inferences, connections, reflections)
1. "An airplane had flown into one of the Twin Towers. Emily and her classmates quickly evacuated their school."	*I found it interesting that the students evacuated. I would think it could have been safer inside the building than on the streets. This reminded me of the novel* Up From the Sea *where during the tsunami in Japan the children ran from their school, and I thought the same thing.*

Figure 10.3.

which will be the last discussion meeting. Book club members collaboratively plan their reading schedule based on the number of pages and chapters in their books and the number of class meetings. The number of pages or chapters for the first meeting are assigned.

6. In classes that have time remaining, students begin independently reading their novels for their first meeting.

Day 3—Book Club Meeting #1

1. Focus Lesson: Setting (time and place of the action) and details such as dialect, customs, clothing, and such that authors use to establish setting are taught through the gradual release of responsibility model with a whole-class short text such as a poem, short story, or an excerpt for the teacher model and guided practice, and an independent application based on the text read for the current book club meeting in preparation for that meeting. For more advanced grade levels, the lesson can also include the use of setting to create mood.

   This lesson emphasizes the importance of setting in these particular novels and asks students to predict what might be the difference in a novel about the events of 9/11 set in 2001, in 2016, on 9/11, before 9/11, after 9/11, and in New York City, in Florida, or elsewhere.

2. Book Club Meetings—Directions:
   - Students are to move into their book clubs to begin the book club meetings.
   - Have your novels and response journals with your discussion questions on your desks.

- Begin with the person whose birthday is closest to January 1 (or another prompt).
- That first person asks his/her discussion question, and everyone answers. Remember to take turns and listen to everyone's answers. If you agree, tell why or extend the answer; if you disagree, use respectful disagreement language.
- Clockwise, the next person shares their discussion question.
- After you discuss everyone's questions, conduct a conversation about the setting and how the author depicts time and place.
- Add any new information about the events of 9/11 to your KWHLR chart in the What I Learned column and reflect on that information in your Reflection column.
- Make any necessary adjustments to your reading schedule for your next meeting.

3. Sharing through Inter–Book Club Meetings—Directions:
   - In your book club, number off 1, 2, 3, 4, 5.
   - All the 1's, the 2's, the 3's, the 4's, and the 5's will each meet in groups.
   - In your inter–book clubs, compare your novels' settings.
4. Students move back to their seats, individually fill out their meeting reflection sheet (see chapter 5), and hand in their meeting reflections with their reader response journal for the current meeting. In classes where there is time, students independently read their novels while the teacher confers with students.
5. Homework—Directions:
   - For your next book club meeting, read to the page number designated by your book club.
   - Fill out your reader response journal; compose a discussion question, following the class guidelines for a "good discussion" question.

Day 4—Book Club Meeting #2

1. Focus Lesson: Characterization (the personality traits of the characters and the means by which an author establishes the character of the characters). Depending on the grade level and the students' experience with literary element lessons, this lesson can include direct and indirect characterization, round and flat characters, and/or static and dynamic characters, and how character may impact goals and decisions.

   The focus lesson is taught through the gradual release of responsibility model with a whole-class short text such as a poem, short story, or an excerpt for the teacher model and guided practice, and an independent application based on the text read for the current book club meeting in preparation for that meeting.

2. Book Club Meetings—Directions:
   - Students are to move into their book clubs to begin the book club meetings.
   - Have your novels and response journals on your desks.
   - Begin with the person whose birthday is closest to, but not after, December 31.
   - That first person asks his/her discussion question, and everyone answers. Remember to take turns and listen to everyone's answers. If you agree, tell why or extend the answer; if you disagree, use respectful disagreement language.
   - Clockwise, the next person shares their discussion question.
   - After you discuss everyone's questions, hold a conversation about the characters that have been introduced and their character traits.
     i. Discuss how the author reveals characters' personalities to the reader.
     ii. Compare/contrast the characters in your novel.
     iii. Predict how you think the characters will each handle problems.
   - Add any new information about the events of 9/11 to your KWHLR chart in the What I Learned column and reflect on that information in your Reflection column.
   - Make any necessary adjustments to your reading schedule for your next meeting.

3. Sharing through Inter–Book Club Meetings—Directions:
   - Students from each book club are to meet in their inter–book club groups.
   - Compare your novels' characters and their traits.

4. Students move back to their seats, individually fill out their meeting reflection sheet, and hand in their meeting reflections with their reader response journal for today's meeting. In classes where there is time, students independently read their novel while the teacher confers with students.

5. Homework—Directions:
   - For your next book club meeting, read to the page number designated by your book club.
   - Fill out your reader response journal (including one journal entry about the characters and their traits and goals) and compose a good discussion question.

Day 5—Book Club Meeting #3

1. Focus Lesson: Conflict (any struggle between opposing forces). In some of the 9/11 novels, there are multiple main characters with multiple conflicts, or they may share the same conflict. For students with prior knowledge of conflict, teachers can present a more advanced lesson on internal and external conflicts.
2. Book Club Meetings—Directions:
   - Students are to move into their book clubs to begin the book club meetings.
   - Have your novels and response journals on your desks.
   - Begin with the person who has not started a discussion and whose last initial is closest to the letter A.
   - Each asks his/her discussion question, and everyone answers. Remember
     i.   to take turns,
     ii. to listen to everyone's answers,
     iii. that if you agree tell why or extend the answer, and
     iv. that if you disagree, use respectful disagreement language.
   - After you discuss everyone's discussion question, discuss
     i.   the problems/challenges/conflicts the characters encountered,
     ii. how the characters handled or mishandled conflicts, and
     iii. how each character is/was affected by the events of 9/11.
   - Add any new information about the events of 9/11 to your KWHLR chart in the What I Learned column and reflect on that information in your Reflection column.
   - Make any necessary adjustments to your reading schedule for your next meeting.
3. Sharing through Inter–Book Club Meetings—Directions:
   - Students from each book club are to meet in their inter–book club groups.
   - In your inter–book clubs, compare problems/conflicts your characters are facing.
4. Students move back to their seats, individually fill out their meeting reflection sheet, and hand in their meeting reflections with their reader response journal for today's meeting. In classes where there is time, students independently read their novel while the teacher confers with students.
5. Homework—Directions:
   - For your next book club meeting, read to the pages designated by your book club.

- Fill out your reader response journal (including one journal entry about the characters and their traits and goals) and compose a good discussion question.

Day 6—Book Club Meeting #4

1. Focus Lesson: Climax (or decisions that the main characters make that lead to or determine the resolution). Using the gradual release of responsibility format, the teacher and then students analyze decisions made by characters in short stories the class has read together, in popular movies, or in narrative poems, such as "Casey at the Bat."
2. Book Club Meetings—Directions:
   - Students are to move into their book clubs to begin the book club meetings.
   - Have your novels and response journals on your desks.
   - Begin with the person who has not already started a discussion and is the tallest.
   - Each member asks his/her discussion question, and everyone answers.
   - After the members discuss everyone's discussion question, discuss the following questions:
     i.   How did the characters handle or mishandle conflicts?
     ii. What decisions did they make? Were those good decisions? Why or why not?
     iii. What was the *effect* of those decisions? How might those decisions lead to a resolution?
     iv. Have you ever had to make those types of decisions?
   - Add any new information about the events of 9/11 to your KWHLR chart in the What I Learned column and reflect on that information in your Reflection column.
   - Plan to finish reading your novel for the next meeting.
3. Sharing through Inter–Book Club Meetings—Directions:
   - Students from each book club are to meet in their inter–book club groups.
   - In your inter–book clubs, compare decisions your characters made and why they made them.
4. Students move back to their seats, individually fill out their meeting reflection sheet, and hand in their meeting reflections with their reader response journal for today's meeting. In classes where there is time, students independently read their novel while the teacher confers with students.

5. Homework—Directions:
   - For your next book club meeting, finish reading your book.
   - Fill out your reader response journal including one journal entry about the ending of the book and the resolution of the conflict(s) and compose a good discussion question.

Day 7—Book Club Meeting #5

1. Focus Lesson: Resolution (how the conflict is resolved). Using the gradual release of responsibility format, the teacher and then students discuss the resolutions made by characters in short stories the class has read together or in popular movies or in narrative poems, such as "Casey at the Bat," and analyze how the resolutions were driven by the decisions made by the characters.

   For classes that have prior learning of the concept of "resolution," a lesson can be added on "denouement" (the final outcome of the story where any loose ends are tied up; the denouement can be an epilogue); however, not every novel will have a denouement.

2. Book Club Meetings—Directions:
   - Students are to move into their book clubs to begin the book club meetings.
   - Have your novels and response journals on your desks.
   - Begin with the person who has not started a discussion or, if all members have had a turn, the person with the first name that comes last alphabetically.
   - Each member asks his/her discussion question, and everyone answers.
   - After you discuss everyone's discussion question, discuss the following:
     i. How did the novel end? What did each book club member think of that?
     ii. Was there any denouement? If not, what would a good "after" chapter contain?
   - Add any new information about the events of 9/11 to your KWHLR chart in the What I Learned column and reflect on that information in your Reflection column.

3. Sharing through Inter–Book Club Meetings—Directions:
   - Students from each book club are to meet in their inter–book club groups.
   - In your inter–book clubs, compare the resolutions of your novels.

4. Students move back to their seats, individually fill out their meeting reflection sheet, and hand in their meeting reflections with their reader response journal for today's meeting.
5. If there is a lot of time left in class, the teacher can begin presenting the Day 8 lesson on after-reading book club presentations (see chapter 6).

In some classes, students individually worked on short book reviews as individual summative assessments (see chapter 7).

Day 8—After-Reading Presentations: Introduction
1. The teacher presents a lesson (or the remainder of the lesson) on after-reading synthesis and ideas for book club presentations (see chapter 6).
2. The students meet in their book clubs and discuss the type of presentation that would best fit their novel and their personalities, interests, and skills.
3. The students write out the plotline, combine and condense their journal chapter summaries, or create a storyboard of their novel. They can divide and assign the chapters among the members.
4. Homework—Directions:
   • Complete your novel summaries.
   • Come to your next meeting with ideas for your presentation and supplies that you will need, if any.

Day 9—After-Reading Presentations: Planning
1. The teacher presents a short lesson on public speaking skills and techniques.
2. Book clubs work on their collaborative components of their presentations and plan any choreography or choral techniques or work on the technology aspects of presentations.
3. As homework, book club members work on the individual elements of their presentations.

Day 10—After-Reading Presentations: Practice
1. Book club members serve as a peer response group for individual writings, such as "I Am" poems.
2. Book clubs finish preparing their presentations and practice.
3. Book clubs each present their after-reading presentations based on their novels.
4. The audience members add any new information learned about the events of 9/11 to their KWHLR charts in the What I Learned column

I am Sergio, a boy who lives in Brooklyn.
I wonder what it would be like to see my mother; she died when I was small.
I hear my grandmother fighting with my dad as he tries to take my prize.
I see the man on the subway collapse when trying to pull the doors open.
I want Gideon, the firefighter who saved the man, to be my real dad.
I am a boy who has no friends and little family.

I pretend the Twin Towers never collapsed.
I feel the ashes from the Towers blow past my face.
I touch the gate when I climb up, trying to see the Towers—or what's left.
I worry about Gideon being safe as he helps the people in the Towers.
I cry because my dad is gone and my mother left me, alone and homeless, at age three.
I am lucky to live with my grandmother whom I love.

I understand that the Twin Towers didn't collapse by accident.
I think about everyone who died on September 11, 2001.
I dream about living a normal life in a peaceful city.
I try to forgive my dad at the 9/11 ceremony.
I hope that terrorists never hurt our country again.
I am Sergio, a boy with many dreams, a grandmother who helps me achieve them,
    and new friend, Gideon.

Figure 10.4.

and reflect on that information in the Reflection column. The class discusses what they learned through the book clubs and their novels.

Note: In one middle-grade class, all the book clubs decided to create and present "I Am" poems for the characters in their novels. The advantage was that the teacher was able not only to grade students individually on the content in their poems and their public speaking skills but also had the option to incorporate group presentation points for collaboration, choreography, and choral techniques.

Figure 10.4 is a student sample for the character Sergio from *Nine, Ten: A September 11 Story* by Nora Raleigh Baskin.

In an eighth-grade class, all book clubs presented summaries of their novel, some through raps and narrative poetry, against a projected background of images and music.

Complementary Novels for Extension Study

To connect the events of 9/11 to other world events or to illustrate the repercussions of the events of 9/11, some novels are suggested for whole-class reading following the book club unit:

- *Up from the Sea* by Leza Lowitz (grades 5–12) is a novel in free verse about the March 11, 2011, earthquake and resulting tsunami in Japan. Kai, a half Japanese, half American seventeen-year-old, has lost his mother, his grandparents, and one of his best friends and is given the opportunity to go to New York City on the tenth anniversary of 9/11 where he will spend some time with young adults who lost their parents as teens in the 9/11 attacks. This novel would serve as an effective continuation to a 9/11 study.

- *The Day of the Pelican* by Katherine Paterson (grades 5–8) relates the story of Melia and her family members, Albanians living in Kosovo, who become homeless refugees from the Serbian oppressors. When they are brought to America, the events of 9/11 impact this Muslim family.
- *Out of Nowhere* by Maria Padian (grades 9–12) is a story about the ways life in a small Maine town, which has become a secondary migration location for Somali refugees, quickly becomes disrupted after the events of 9/11. The Somali high school students face bigotry and even hostility from not only their classmates but also from teachers and townspeople. Four Somali students turn the soccer team into a winning team, but it is still difficult for them to gain respect for their culture, beliefs, and traditions.

Adaptations for Social Studies/History Classes

When teaching this unit in social studies/history classes, the focus lessons would center on the social studies curriculum and standards, such as

- the history leading to the September 11, 2001, events;
- conflict in the Middle East;
- the consequences and effects of the events of 9/11, in the United States and globally;
- the historical context of terrorism;
- the impact of terrorist activities on the United States;
- past and current U.S. foreign policy in the Middle East;
- the post-9/11 war in Afghanistan; and
- stereotyping and Islamophobia.

The social studies/history curriculum may not make allowance for the amount of time allotted to the unit described in this chapter. In these cases, book clubs can meet twice a week, Mondays and Thursdays or Tuesdays and Fridays, dividing the novels into four readings rather than five or six. Teachers may well plan history focus lessons that are longer than the typical ten-to-fifteen-minute Reading Workshop focus lessons, allowing little or no time for in-class reading.

Additionally, the presentations in these classes would be more effective if they are connected to the social studies curriculum, possibly requiring additional student research. For example, based on the novel *Towers Falling* by Jewell Parker Rhodes, a presentation titled "Ten Years After," could be staged as a news interview show highlighting information about PTSD, sharing statistics from the 9/11 attacks, and featuring interviews with some of the characters from the novels. For the novel *Nine, Ten: A September 11 Story*, a presentation could focus on "Events Leading Up to 9/11" with students including historic events as well as events from the novel.

In these ways, a 9/11 novel study, read through book clubs, would enhance the curricular study and aid in meeting social studies/history standards in upper elementary school, middle school, and high school. This unit can also be adapted employing novels to study other historic events.

Appendix

Reproducible Forms

Figure 4A.1. Book Club Meeting Agenda

BOOK CLUB MEETING AGENDA

1. After the focus lesson, Club members pull your desks into circles (if your desks are not already positioned in Clubs)

2. Take your **book** and your **completed Reader Response** to your group.

3. Distribute Reader Response sheets from last meeting that are on one of your desks and add to your Reading Journals.

4. 25 minutes: Using texts and notes, discuss the assigned reading. following suggestions for supportive, productive discussions and listening [see charts].

5. Starting with the person who...[listen for the day's suggestion], discuss each member's discussion question. You may not cover all questions because some of the questions elicited so much talk that time ran out.

6. Integrate the day's *Focus Lesson* into your discussion.

7. When finished, make any necessary adjustments to your reading schedule.

8. Collect Reader Response journals, take to HomeWork bin, and distribute Meeting Reflection forms.

9. Share something from your meeting: a social skill that was implemented well; an insight about your text; a way you employed the focus lesson.

10. Move desks back to position and *individually* fill out Meeting Reflection sheets as specifically as possible. Comments will be kept confidential. This will be your ticket out the door.

11. Continue reading your text until the end of the period.

Figure 5A.1.   Book Club Meeting Reflection Form

TEXT CLUB MEETING REFLECTION (Write neatly)

Name_____   Text Title _____

The Text

Today we discussed _____

_____

From our discussion I learned _____

_____

An interesting point made was _____

_____

A question I still have about the text — or — What I want to find out now is _____

_____

_____

The Meeting – Social Skills

I felt that the meeting went _____ because _____

_____

_____

+ What I did well today   — What I need to work on   = What I tried

___ being prepared   ___ listening   ___actively paticipating   ___ supporting others

___ respectful disagreeing   ___ agreeing and extending   ___ piggybacking on other ideas

___ turn-taking   ___ including all group members   ____ making eye contact with speakers

---

Figure 5A.2. Book Club Basic Journal, page 1

Name _____ Text _____

TEXT CLUB Response Journal

For Meeting Date _____ Chapters _____to_____ Pages_____to _____

Summary- list important events; highlight new characters introduced

- _____
- _____
- _____
- _____
- _____
- _____
- _____
- _____
- _____
- _____
- _____
- _____

A Good Discussion Question—A question that will generate conversation and encourage different points of view and ideas

_____

_____

_____

_____

_____

Sample Response Starters to begin Reflections:

I noticed...	I was really surprised...because...	I am guessing that...because...
I began to think...	Something new I learned ...	What I found interesting...
I like the way...	This reminds me of ...because...	A question I have...because...
My favorite part was...	I think ...is important becaue...	I wonder why...
I think the author...	When I read..., it made me feel...	What I think will happen is...

Figure 5A.3. Book Club Basic Journal, page 2

Stop every 1/3 as you read and jot a personal response on what you are thinking about the text.

Reflection #1 on what I read in these chapters [Begin with a Response Starter on page 1]

_____

_____

_____

_____

_____

_____

_____

_____

Reflection #2 on what I read in these chapters [Begin with a Response Starter on page 1]

_____

_____

_____

_____

_____

_____

_____

Reflection #3 on what I read in these chapters:

_____

_____

_____

_____

_____

_____

_____

_____

_____

Figure 5A.4. Book Club Basic Double-Entry Journal

Name _____	Text Title _____
My Notes for Our Next Text Club Meeting Pages _____ to _____	

Something I noticed in the novel (page #) (a character, something about the setting, an event, a decision, a quote from the text)	What I am thinking about that... (inferences, connections, reflections)
1.	
2.	
3.	

A discussion question—one that will generate conversation and encourage different opinions/points of view:

My answer to my question:

Figure 5A.5. Book Club Advanced Double-Entry Journal, page 1

Name _____ Text _____

TEXT CLUB Double-Entry Journal

For Meeting Date _____ Chapters _____to_____ Pages_____to _____

Summary—list the main events from the chapters read in bullet points; highlight new characters

- _____
- _____
- _____
- _____
- _____
- _____
- _____
- _____
- _____
- _____
- _____

Discussion Question—and my thoughts about the question and answer to the question:

_____
_____
_____
_____
_____
_____
_____
_____

Figure 5A.6. Book Club Advanced Double-Entry Journal, to be used with Book Club Advanced Double-Entry Journal, page 1

From **the TEXT**:	From **my THOUGHTS**:
1.Interesting Quote from the reading	My thoughts about the quote:
2. Setting—Time/Place/Mood/Description	My thoughts about Setting and its effect
3. Character, new or important, ansd traits :	My thoughts about that Character
4. An Event or Information from the Text	My Inference or Prediction based on that info:

Figure 5A.7. Book Club Double-Entry Character Journal, to be used with Book Club Advanced Double-Entry Journal, page 1

From the **TEXT**:	My Thoughtful Reflection:
1.A Character and His/Her Character Traits	What I am thinking about that:
2. Problem the Character is Facing	What I am thinking about that :
3.How the Character is (Mis)Handling Problem	What I am thinking about that:
4. Motivatons for Character's Actions	What I am thinking about that:

Figure 5A.8. Book Club Double-Entry Varied Topics Journal, to be used with Book Club Advanced Double-Entry Journal, page 1

From the **TEXT**:	My Thoughtful Reflection:
1.Discussion Question or Point:	What I Am Thinking About That
2. Quote or Main Character & Traits	What I Am Thinking About That
3. Vocabulary/Interesting Word, Definition, and Sentence it appeared in:	What I Am Thinking About That
4. A Question, Inference, or Prediction	What I Am Thinking About That

© Lesley Roessing, 2019

Figure 6A.1. Book Club Presentation Rubric

Book Club Presentation Rubric

Book Club _____   Member_____

Content (Group Points)

____/10 pts Introduction, including author, title, genre

____/05 pts Narration to connect the scenes, objects, or presentation components

____/55 pts Literary Elements included:

    ____/10 pts all major characters

    ____/05 pts crucial setting(s)

    ____/40 pts plot elements: inciting incident, conflict, climax, resolution

____/10 pts Media: appropriate choreography/choral techniques, multi-media components, objects, costumes, or other supplemental features

____/05 pts Conclusion: a brief review of the novel and what you learned from the novel

Public Speaking (Individual Points)

____/05 pts articulation: enunciation, pronunciation, and projection

____/05 pts body stance: facing audience, natural gestures (unless choreographed movement), and movement (still feet, except for choreographed movement)

____/05 pts oral skills: volume, pitch, pacing, intonation, expression

____/100 pts

Comments:

Figure 7A.1. Sample Book Club Book Review Rubric

Sample Book Club Book Review Rubric

Novel Title _____ Member_____

NOVEL REVIEW:

____/10 pts   Introduction, including essential elements: author, title, publisher, copyright date

____/20 pts   Short Summary, 1-paragraph which includes all major characters, setting, and plot elements: exposition, inciting incident, conflict, climax, resolution

____/50 pts   Opinion, 1-2 paragraphs:

        _____/30 pts Your critical analysis of the novel (or the assigned novel element)

        _____/20 pts Text evidence and quotes, supporting views (include page numbers)

____/05 pts   Conclusion: Summarizing statement about novel or statement about the theme

WRITING:

____/10 pts   Style writing lesson taught in focus lesson: Word Choice, Sentence Fluency, or Voice (Ideas and Organization are included in the Review points above)

____/05 pts   Editing: Spellchecked and Proofread

_____/100 pts Total

Comments:

© Lesley Roessing, 2019

Figure 8A.1. Book Club Double-Entry Author's Craft Journal

Responses to Author's Craft

Copy from your novel examples of good, effective, or innovative writing, such as
- detailed, sensory descriptions of characters or settings
- authentic-sounding dialogue, use of dialect, jargon, or regional accent
- interesting use of punctuation or word order
- attention-grabbing words or unusual phrases or words used in interesting ways
- figurative language
- something particular to this author's writing that is effective or thought-provoking
- a craft or technique we have studied in Writing Workshop

From the TEXT – Page #	Technique Identification & My THOUGHTS
1.	
2.	
3.	

Figure 9A.1.   Informational Text Club Double-Entry Journal

Name _____   Text Title _____

My Notes for Our Next Text Club Meeting   Pages _____ to _____

A FACT I read	What I am thinking about that... (inferences, connections, reflections)
1.	
2.	
3.	
4.	

A discussion question—one that will generate conversation and encourage different opinions/points of view:

References

General

Carr, P. B., and Walton, G. M. (2014). Cues of working together fuel intrinsic motivation. *Journal of Experimental Social Psychology*, 53, 169–184.

Graham, S., and Hebert, M. A. (2010). *Writing to read: Evidence for how writing can improve reading. A Carnegie Corporation time to act report.* Washington, DC: Alliance for Excellent Education.

Long, L. H., and Roessing, L. (2015). What are book clubs doing in *health* class? *ALAN Review*, 43(1), 69–77.

Roessing, L. (2007). Making research matter. *English Journal*, 96(4), 50–55.

Roessing, L. (2009). *The write to read: Response journals that increase comprehension.* Thousand Oaks, CA: Corwin Press.

Roessing, L. (2012). *No more "us" and "them": Classroom lessons and activities to promote peer respect.* Lanham, MD: Rowman & Littlefield.

Roessing, L. (2014). *Bridging the gap: Reading critically and writing meaningfully to get to the core.* Lanham, MD: Rowman & Littlefield.

Strauss, K. (2016). These are the skills bosses say new college grads do not have. *Forbes.* Retrieved from https://www.forbes.com/sites/karstenstrauss/2016/05/17/these-are-the-skills-bosses-say-new-college-grads-do-not-have/#391d6f054916.

Resources and Texts Cited in Chapters

Chapter 2

Hamilton, B. (2006). *Soul surfer: A true story of faith, family, and fighting to get back on the board.* New York, NY: MTV Books.

Chapter 5
National Reading Panel (U.S.), & National Institute of Child Health and Human Development (U.S.). (2000). *Report of the National Reading Panel: Teaching children to read: An evidence-based assessment of the scientific research literature on reading and its implications for reading instruction: reports of the subgroups.* Washington, DC: National Institute of Child Health and Human Development, National Institutes of Health.

Chapter 6
Cerra, K. O. (2016). *Just a drop of water.* New York, NY: Sky Pony.
Creech, S. (2016). *Moo.* New York, NY: Joanna Cotler Books.
Holt, K. A. (2014). *Rhyme schemer.* San Francisco, CA: Chronicle Books.
Hughes, L. (1996). Thank you, ma'am. In F. Safier (Ed.), *Impact: 50 short short stories.* New York, NY: Holt, McDougal.
Jacobson, J. R. (2018). *The dollar kids.* Somerville, MA: Candlewick Press.
Miklowitz, G. D. (1986). *The war between the classes.* New York, NY: Laurel Leaf.
Perkins, C. (1955). Blue suede shoes. On *Blue suede shoes* [Vinyl record]. Memphis, TN: Sun Records.

Chapter 8
Anderson, L. H., and Carroll, E. (2018). *Speak, the graphic novel.* New York, NY: Farrar, Straus & Giroux.
Atwater, R., and Atwater, F. (1992). *Mr. Popper's penguins.* New York, NY: Little, Brown.
Austen, J., Sach, L., and Nagulakonda, R. (2013). *Pride and prejudice: The graphic novel.* New York, NY: Campfire.
Avi. (2003). *Nothing but the truth.* New York, NY: Orchard.
Bauer, M. D. (2012). *Little dog lost.* New York, NY: Atheneum Books for Young Readers.
Bell, C. (2014). *El Deafo.* New York, NY: Harry N. Abrams.
Creech, S. (2003). *Love that dog.* New York, NY: Scholastic.
Creech, S. (2016). *Moo.* New York, NY: Joanna Cotler Books.
Crew, D. (1998). *Bigmama's.* New York, NY: Greenwillow Books.
Dahl, Roald. (2006). *Skin and other stories.* New York: Puffin Books.
Dean, C. (2012). *Forget me not.* New York, NY: Simon Pulse.
DeCamillo, Kate. (2001). *Because of winn-dixie.* Somerville, MA: Candlewick Press.
dePaola, T. (2002). *26 Fairmount avenue.* New York, NY: Puffin Books.
Engle, M. (2012). *The wild book.* New York, NY: Harcourt Children's Books.
Engle, M. (2015). *Enchanted air.* New York, NY: Atheneum Books for Young Readers.
Engle, M. (2019). *Soaring earth.* New York, NY: Atheneum Books for Young Readers.
Erlich, A. (Ed.). (2001). *When I was your age: Original stories about growing up* (Vols. 1–2). Somerville, MA: Candlewick Press.

Fletcher, R. (2005). *Marshfield dreams: When I was a kid*. New York, NY: Holt.

Grimes, N. (2016). *Garvey's choice*. Honesdale, PA: WordSong.

Hale, S. (2017). *Real friends*. Huntsville, AL: First Second.

Hall, M. K., and Jones, C. (Eds.). (2011). *Dear bully: Seventy authors tell their stories*. New York, NY: HarperTeen.

Holt, K. A. (2014). *Rhyme schemer*. San Francisco, CA: Chronicle Books.

Holt, K. A. (2015). *House arrest*. San Francisco, CA: Chronicle Books.

Horowitz, A., Johnston, A., Damerum, K., and Takasaki, Y. (2006). *Stormbreaker: The graphic novel*. New York, NY: Philomel Books.

Jacobson, J. R. (2018). *The dollar kids*. Somerville, MA: Candlewick Press.

Jensen, C., and Morrison, L. (2018). *Every shiny thing*. New York, NY: Abrams/Amulet Books.

Koertge, Ron. (2006). *Shakespeare bats cleanup*. Somerville, MA: Candlewick Press.

Krosoczka, J. J. (2018). *Hey, kiddo*. Huntsville, AL: Graphia.

Laminack, L. (2004). *Saturdays and teacakes*. Atlanta, GA: Peachtree.

Lee, H., and Fordham, F. (2018). *To kill a mockingbird: A graphic novel*. New York, NY: HarperCollins.

Lee, S. (2015). *Amazing fantastic incredible: A marvelous memoir*. New York, NY: Touchstone.

McCafferty, M. (Ed.). (2004). *Sixteen: Stories about that sweet and bitter birthday*. New York, NY: Broadway Books.

Messner, Kate. (2018). *Breakout*. New York: Bloomsbury.

Meyer, S., and Young, K. (2010). *Twilight: The graphic novel* (Vol. 1). New York, NY: Yen Press.

Myers, Walter Dean. (2001). *145th Street: short stories*. New York: Laurel Leaf.

Miklowitz, G. D. (1986). *The war between the classes*. New York, NY: Laurel Leaf.

Mochizuki, K. (2002). *Passage to freedom: The Sugihara story*. New York, NY: Lee & Low Books.

Myers, W. D. (2004). *Monster*. New York, NY: Amistad.

Myers, W. D., and Sims, G. A. (2015). *Monster: A graphic novel*. New York, NY: Amistad.

Naidoo, B. (2002). *Out of bounds: Seven stories of conflict and hope*. Chicago, IL: Klett.

Park, Linda Sue. (2010). *A Long walk to water*. Boston, MA: Clarion Books.

Parton, D. (1996). *Coat of many colors*. New York, NY: HarperCollins.

Polacco, P. (1993). *Some birthday!* New York, NY: Simon & Schuster/Paula Wiseman Books.

Polacco, P. (1996). *Meteor*. New York, NY: Puffin Books.

Polacco, P. (1997). *Thunder cake*. St. Louis, MO: Turtleback Books.

Polacco, P. (1998). *My rotten redheaded older brother*. New York, NY: Simon & Schuster/Paula Wiseman Books.

Polacco, P. (1999). *My ol' man*. New York, NY: Puffin Books.

Polacco, P. (2001). *Thank you, Mr. Falkner*. New York, NY: Philomel Books.

Polacco, P. (2010). *The junkyard wonders*. New York, NY: Philomel Books.

Polacco, P. (2015). *An "A" from Miss Keller.* New York, NY: Putnam's Sons Books for Young Readers.

Polisner, G. (2016). *The memory of things.* New York, NY: Wednesday Books.

Prince, L. (2014). *Tomboy: A graphic memoir.* San Francisco, CA: Zest Books.

Rylant, C. (1993). *When I was young in the mountains.* New York, NY: Puffin Books.

Satrapi, M. (2004). *Persepolis: The story of a childhood.* New York, NY: Pantheon.

Shovan, L. (2016). *The last fifth grade of Emerson Elementary.* New York, NY: Wendy Lamb Books/Random House.

Sones, S. (2019). *Stop pretending: What happened when my big sister went crazy.* New York, NY: HarperTeen.

Sternburg, J. (2011). *Like pickle juice on a cookie.* New York, NY: Abrams.

Telgemeier, R. (2010). *Smile.* New York, NY: Scholastic/Graphix.

Telgemeier , R. (2014). *Sisters.* New York, NY: Scholastic/Graphix.

Terry, E. (2017). *Forget me not.* New York, NY: Feiwel & Friends.

Thrush, M. (2015). *Honor girl: A graphic memoir.* Somerville, MA: Candlewick Press.

Twain, M., Mann, R., and Kumar, N. (2010). *The adventures of Huckleberry Finn.* New York, NY: Campfire.

Wissinger, T. W. (2013). *Gone fishing: A novel in verse.* New York, NY: Houghton Mifflin Books for Children.

Woodson, J. (2004). *Locomotion.* New York, NY: Speak.

Woodson, J. (2014). *Brown girl dreaming.* New York, NY: Nancy Paulsen Books.

Chapter 9

Anderson, L. H. (2000). *Fever, 1793.* New York, NY: Aladdin.

Beah, I. (2007). *Long way gone: Memoirs of a boy soldier.* New York, NY: Farrar, Straus & Giroux.

Choldenko, G. (2015). *Chasing secrets.* New York, NY: Random House.

Cooney, C. (2005). *Code orange.* New York, NY: Delacorte Press.

Courtenay, B. (1996). *The power of one.* New York, NY: Ballantine Books.

Deuker, C. (2007). *Gym candy.* New York, NY: HMH Books for Young Readers.

Efaw, A. (2010). *After.* New York, NY: Speak.

Friend, N. (2004). *Perfect: A novel.* Minneapolis, MN: Milkweed Editions.

Gordon, S. (1996). *Waiting for the rain.* New York, NY: Laurel Leaf.

Gottlieb, L. (2001). *Stick figure: A diary of my former self.* East Rutherford, NJ: Berkley.

Hiaasen, C. (2005). *Flush.* New York, NY: Knopf Books for Young Readers.

Hiaasen, C. (2006). *Hoot.* New York, NY: Yearling Books.

Hiaasen, C. (2009). *Scat.* New York, NY: Knopf Books for Young Readers.

Hiaasen, C. (2012). *Chomp.* New York, NY: Knopf Books for Young Readers.

Hiaasen, C. (2018). *Squirm.* New York, NY: Knopf Books for Young Readers.

Hopkinson, D. (2013). *The great trouble: A mystery of London, the Blue Death, and a boy called Eel.* New York, NY: Knopf.

Humphreys, J. D. (2015). *Child soldier: When boys and girls are used in war.* Toronto, ON: Kids Can Press.

Johnson, A. (2005). *The first part last.* New York, NY: Simon Pulse.

Korman, G. (2009). *Pop.* New York, NY: Balzer + Bray.

Lucier, M. (2014). *A death-struck year.* New York, NY: HMH Books.

MacKel, K. (2008). *Boost.* New York, NY: Dial Books.

Mathabane, M. (1998). *Kaffir boy: An autobiography.* New York, NY: Free Press.

Mikaelson, B. (2005). *Tree girl.* New York, NY: HarperTeen.

Naidoo, B. (1993). *Chain of fire.* New York, NY: HarperCollins.

Park, L. S. (2010). *A long walk to water: Based on a true story.* New York, NY: Clarion Books.

Paterson, K. (2007). *The day of the pelican.* New York, NY: Farrar, Straus & Giroux.

Paton, A. (2003). *Cry, the beloved country.* New York, NY: Scribner.

Powers, J. L. (2011). *This thing called the future.* El Paso, TX: Cinco Puntos Press.

Raina, A. (2016). *When morning comes.* Vancouver, BC: Tradewind Books.

Schneider, R. (2015). *Extraordinary means.* New York, NY: HarperCollins/Katherine Tegen.

Sierra, Judy. (1992). *Cinderella.* Santa Barbara, CA: Greenwood.

Sparks, B. (2004). *Annie's baby: The diary of Anonymous, a pregnant teenager.* New York, NY: HarperTeen.

Chapter 10

Baskin, N. R. (2016). *Nine, ten: A September 11 story.* New York, NY: Scholastic.

Cerra, K. O. (2016). *Just a drop of water.* New York, NY: Sky Pony.

Donwerth-Chikamatsu, A. (2016). *Somewhere among.* New York, NY: Atheneum.

Ellerbee, L. (2011). What happened: The story of September 11, 2011 [Television series episode]. In *Nick News with Linda Ellerbee.* Retrieved from https://www.you tube.com/watch?v=F-dhyzaeB1Y.

Lowitz, L. (2016). *Up from the sea.* New York, NY: Ember.

Maynard, J. (2004). *The usual rules.* New York, NY: St. Martin's Press.

Mills, W. (2016). *All we have left.* New York, NY: Bloomsbury.

Modigliani, L. (2011). I was 11 on 9/11. *Scholastic News Edition 5/6.* Retrieved from http://www.scholastic.com/browse/article.jsp?id=3756391.

Padian, M. (2013). *Out of nowhere.* New York, NY: Knopf Books for Young Readers.

Paterson, K. (2009). *The day of the pelican.* New York, NY: Sandpiper.

Polisner, G. (2016). *The memory of things.* New York, NY: Wednesday Books.

Rhodes, J. P. (2016). *Towers falling.* New York, NY: Little, Brown.

Rogers, T. (2014). *Eleven.* Los Angeles, CA: Alto Nido.

Stine, C. (2005). *Refugees.* New York, NY: Delacorte Books for Young Readers.

~

About the Author

Lesley Roessing taught middle school English-language arts and humanities for twenty years before becoming the founding director of the Coastal Savannah Writing Project and senior lecturer in the College of Education at Armstrong State University (now Georgia Southern University). At the university, she worked with K–12 teachers in all disciplines and taught courses in literacy to pre-service and in-service teachers. She currently serves as literacy consultant for a K–8 school.

Ms. Roessing has published four professional books for educators: *The Write to Read: Response Journals That Increase Comprehension; Comma Quest: The Rules They Followed—the Sentences They Saved; No More "Us" and "Them": Classroom Lessons and Activities to Promote Peer Respect;* and *Bridging the Gap: Reading Critically and Writing Meaningfully to Get to the Core.* She contributed chapters to two anthologies, *Young Adult Literature and the Digital World: Textual Engagement through Visual Literacy* and *Queer Adolescent Literature as a Complement to the English Language Arts Curriculum.* She also served as the editor of *Connections,* the peer-reviewed journal of the Georgia Council of Teachers of English.

Lesley facilitated book clubs in her own high school and middle grade classes and in her undergraduate and graduate classrooms as well as being invited into classrooms at a variety of grade levels and disciplines. She has introduced book club strategies and lessons to K–16 educators through workshops, in-services, and conference presentations.

Made in the USA
Monee, IL
27 November 2020